JAM DROPS
AND
MARBLE CAKE

JAM DROPS AND MARBLE CAKE

60 YEARS OF CWA AWARD-WINNING RECIPES

MURDOCH BOOKS

CONTENTS

ASSOCIATION

SEASIDE HOME APPEAL

Judging at The Land Cookery Competition, 1951. Photo courtesy of the CWA.

INTRODUCTION

Thishis timeless collection of award-winning baking recipes celebrates 60 successful years of a delicious collaboration between *The Land* and the Country Women's Association (CWA) of New South Wales through *The Land* Cookery Competition. This Competition was originally set up in 1951 to raise money for the Seaside Homes Appeal. Nearly 1000 pounds was raised in the first year—a resounding success for the CWA and its fundraising appeal. But the success of this cookery competition was more than financial—in a sense, it validated and celebrated the often unrecognised work of women at the time.

The women who entered the first Competition had precious little to celebrate in the preceding years. They had seen their husbands, sons and brothers go off to fight in World War II—only the lucky ones welcomed them home. They had dealt with isolation and loneliness, and through this they learnt the importance of community. And they all knew the value of family and how to feed them. Their skill with the wooden spoon was born out of necessity, but through the *The Land* Cookery Competition it became cause for celebration.

The State Finals are held in May every year, with the Competition running throughout the state in the preceding 12 months. Every year the CWA issues 'Schedules', outlining the rules of the Competition, the various categories and the prizes up for grabs. Back in 1955, First Prize in Section Two (Buttercakes) was awarded 10 pounds. In 2012, the same prize will win you $50.

Through all the social and political changes of the intervening years, the Competition rules have remained virtually unchanged from their original form, and the rules from 2011–12 may be found on pages 10–11. Throughout wars, droughts, fires and floods, you could always depend on the *The Land* Cookery Competition to uphold that: 'All fruit cakes must observe the 250 g butter basis as a standard mixture for size and weight'. Also, 'in judging, the method of cutting right through the centre of the cake must be observed'. But in 1955, the cakes were able 'to be joined again with Durex tape for semi-finals', one of the few customs wisely deemed better not to preserve!

In the early days of the Competition, contestants used their own repertoire of recipes to bake, taking cue from the rules printed in the annual Schedules. As the Competition grew and gained momentum, specific recipes were published for the contestants to use, a number of them reappearing in the line-up year after year with or without slight variations to the ingredient quantities and method. It is these recipes that you will find within this book. From its genesis, the Competition has been open to any person residing in New South Wales, males and females, town and country dwellers. Now, 60 years after the first *The Land* Cookery Competition, it costs just 40 cents to enter your fruit cake or your fancy biscuits.

Early recipes contained no specifications for the tins—the competitors used whatever they had on hand, be it roasting tin or lamington pan—but in the following we have included recommendations. In the spirit of the Competition and the resourcefulness of the original bakers, we would encourage you to adapt recipes and use the equipment you have available. Often some recipe components, such as icings, have been suggested but not included in the main recipe. In these cases, use your favourite one to embellish your baking, or decorate simply with a dusting of icing sugar.

From jam drops to passionfruit slice, Anzac biscuits (both the original wartime recipe and the embellished recipe from the eighties) to fruit cake, and lamingtons to marble cake, the recipes brought together in this book celebrate our rich heritage of baking and community.

Elaine Armstrong

Elaine Armstrong
State President
Country Women's Association
of New South Wales

Jeuper

John Dwyer
General Manager
The Land

THE LAND

RULES

1. This Contest is conducted by the Country Women's Association of NSW to raise funds for the Association.

2. The Contest is not restricted to members of the CWA; it is open to any person residing in NSW.

3. Entries at Branch level to be accompanied by 40 cents entry fee. Must be made on the printed current 2011–2012 coupon, which will appear fortnightly in The Land newspaper, otherwise they will be disqualified. Each entry requires a separate coupon. Entries must be lodged with the Cookery Officer of a CWA branch and contestants may enter in one Branch and one Group only. Entries in the State Finals must be accompanied by the original coupon.

4. Each Branch conducts its separate contest at any time that is considered suitable. First and Second prize winners must be two different competitors of Branch contest who will then be eligible to enter Group Semi-finals. This is a competition that is conducted from Branch to Group and then to State level, branches cannot enter direct to Group Semi-finals.

5. First prize winners only of Group Semi-Finals are eligible for the State Final conducted concurrently with the CWA Annual General Conference. (This does not apply in Section 6.)

6. Additional classes, other than those on the Schedule, may be included in Branch contests, and additional Prizes awarded locally, but prize winners in such classes will not complete in the Semi-finals or State Finals of the contest.

7. Branches and Groups will appoint their own judges, BUT judges and stewards for the State Finals will be appointed by the CWA State Committee.

2011–12

8. All exhibits entered in this contest (except in Section One, Classes A and B, and Section Seven) may be sold at Branch and Group level. All exhibits (except Section Six) become the property of CWA at State Level.

9. The judges decisions are absolutely final and not to be questioned or discussed with the judges.

10. The 40 cents entry fee with each entry form, plus proceeds of the sales of entries, and any other monies raised at the same function, shall be sent through Group Treasurer to CWA Head Office NOT The Land Office.

11. All entries in the State Finals will be displayed and then sold except Section Six, proceeds of the sale to be added to the Cookery Contest funds for the CWA.

12. No ring tin to be used throughout the contest. NO RACK MARKS ON ENTRIES.

13. NO PACKAGE MIXTURES ARE TO BE USED IN ANY CLASS OF THE CONTEST.

14. Owners may purchase their exhibit, if they inform the Steward when entering their exhibit at State Level.

15. All entries must be accompanied by a complete list of all ingredients used, plus your name, address, "use by date and Product of Australia" at the bottom. IMPORTANT All fruit cakes and sultana cakes must be entered un-iced. ALL FRUIT CAKES MUST OBSERVE the 250g BUTTER BASIS as a standard mixture for size and weight. Tins must be square or round in judging, the method of cutting right through the centre of the cake must be observed. NO CUT CAKE WILL BE ACCEPTED AT STATE FINALS but CAN be entered cut at the Group Semi-finals.

All recipes can be found in the June 2011 journal.

"The Land"
COOKERY CONTEST

£300
IN PRIZES

CONDUCTED FOR THE COUNTRY WOMEN'S ASSOCIATION OF N.S.W.

1962–63 Schedule cover. Image courtesy of the CWA.

BUTTERCAKES AND SPONGES

PLAIN BUTTERCAKE 1

First judged in 1968

Makes: 2 x 20 cm (8 in) round cakes

There must be no fruit, nuts, cherries or peel in or on cake. Must be simply iced on top only, but NOT decorated. Essences may be used if desired. Approximately 2 ½ inch minimum depth of cake is desirable.

Points to be looked for in judging for ALL buttercakes: There should not be any large holes or tunnels. Cakes should not have hard crusts, be sugary or sticky. Cooking should be even right throughout, and the cake should not be crumbly or soggy.

From Schedule of 1969–70

250 g (9 oz) butter, softened
330 g (11¾ oz/1½ cups) sugar
4 eggs
450 g (1 lb/3 cups) self-raising flour
Pinch of salt
250 ml (9 fl oz/1 cup) milk

1   Preheat oven to moderate (180°C/350°F/Gas 4). Grease two deep 20 cm (8 in) round cake tins and line bases with baking paper.

2   Cream butter and sugar until pale and creamy. Add eggs one at a time and beat well after each addition. Add sifted flour and salt alternately with the milk.

3   Divide the batter evenly between the prepared tins. Bake for about 35 minutes.

PLAIN BUTTERCAKE 2

First judged in 1968

Makes: 1 x 20 cm (8 in) round cake

125 g (4½ oz) butter, softened
165 g (5¾ oz/¾ cup) caster sugar
1 teaspoon vanilla essence
2 eggs
450 g (1 lb/3 cups) self-raising flour
125 ml (4 fl oz/½ cup) milk

1 Preheat oven to moderate (180°C/350°F/Gas 4). Grease a deep 20 cm (8 in) round cake tin and line base with baking paper.

2 Cream together butter, sugar and vanilla until pale and creamy. Add eggs one at a time, beating well after each addition. Sift flour and fold in alternately with the milk.

3 Spoon into the prepared tin and bake for 50–60 minutes. Turn out onto a wire rack to cool.

State President Mrs Barber congratulates the winner of the Sponge Sandwich Section, Mrs Knight, of Whitton, July 1963. Photo courtesy of *The Land*.

ORANGE BUTTERCAKE

First judged in 1952

Makes: 1 loaf

Must be iced on top and decorated with grated rind, or rind cut in fancy shapes ONLY. It must be baked in a loaf, deep square or round tin.

Hints to the competitor: Grated rind adds a more definite orange flavour than juice alone.

From Schedule of 1964–65

220 g (7¾ oz) butter, softened
220 g (7¾ oz/1 cup) sugar
Finely grated zest of 1 well-coloured
    orange
3 eggs

Juice of ½ orange
Milk, at room temperature
150 g (5½ oz/1 cup) plain flour
150 g (5½ oz/1 cup) self-raising flour
Orange icing, to serve

1   Preheat oven to moderate (180°C/350°F/Gas 4). Grease and flour a 13 x 23 cm (5 x 9 in) (top measurement) loaf tin.

2   Cream butter and sugar to a cream with orange zest. Add eggs one at a time, beating well after each addition.

3   Squeeze orange juice into a cup. Add enough milk to make up to 185 ml (6 fl oz/¾ cup)—this will curdle, which is good.

4   Take off mixer and gradually add the well-sifted combined flours alternately with the milk and juice mixture. Combine well until smooth.

5   Put into the prepared tin and tap the tin lightly on the bench. Bake for 40–45 minutes or until cooked in an even manner. Turn out to cool. When cold, ice with orange icing.

ORANGE AND POPPY SEED CAKE

First judged in 1988

Makes: 1 x 20 cm (8 in) round cake

50 g (1¾ oz/⅓ cup) poppy seeds
60 ml (2 fl oz/¼ cup) milk
185 g (6½ oz) butter, softened
220 g (7¾ oz/1 cup) caster sugar
Finely grated zest of 1 orange
3 eggs
300 g (10½ oz/2 cups) self-raising flour

125 ml (4 fl oz/½ cup) orange juice

Icing
125 g (4½ oz/1 cup) icing sugar
1 teaspoon butter, softened
2–4 teaspoons hot water

1 Preheat oven to moderate (180°C/350°F/Gas 4). Grease a deep 20 cm (8 in) round cake tin and line base with baking paper. Combine poppy seeds and milk. Stand aside for 1 hour.

2 Cream butter and sugar with orange zest in a bowl until pale and creamy. Add eggs one at a time, beating well after each addition. Fold in the sifted flour alternately with the milk/poppy seed mixture and the orange juice. Pour into the prepared tin.

3 Bake for about 1 hour or until cooked when tested. Stand 5 minutes before turning out.

4 To make the icing, sift icing sugar into a bowl and add butter and enough of the hot water to make a spreading consistency.

5 Ice cooled cake with icing. No decoration.

LAND NEWSPAPER ANNOUNCE BIG INCREASE FOR BRANCH AWARDS IN FUTURE COOKERY CONTESTS

CWA has always been most appreciative of The Land Newspaper's generosity in connection with prizes for our famous "Land Cookery Contest", and at the Annual General Conference further offers were publicised. From next year The Land will increase prize money to $1000, the extra $400 being awarded to branches with the most entries in the local contest.

The announcement was made by Managing Editor of The Land, Mr John Parker, when he presented prizes to winners of the 1972-73 contest in Broken Hill.

The awards would be made in two sections. The first would be open to branches with less than 30 members, and the second to branches with a membership of more than 30.

Miss Greta Winch, Chairman of the Organising Committee said that the response to this year's contest had been amazing, considering the distance most entries had to travel. She said she thought it was equal to any held in Sydney, and the whole thing had proved how increasingly popular the contest is.

A total of 270 branches was represented, and it was the second time ever that the whole 30 Groups of CWA had entered.

Proud moment for Far North-West Group when it received a special trophy from Miss Winch, for being the only Group to achieve 100% participation by all of its branches.

Miss Winch said that it had been a tremendous effort by this Group, especially since all the branches are so scattered and remote.

Sale of the Cookery Contest entries after judging was very popular, a record sum of $485 being raised.

Some changes to apply to the 1973-74 schedule were announced by Miss Winch, these being Grapefuit Jam instead of Strawberry, Lamingtons instead of Pettit Fours, Banana Cake instead of Coffee Walnut Cake, Chocolate Cake instead of Banana Cake for the "under 17 years" section. Miss Winch said that final details on how to organise the contest at Branch Level will be published in The Land in the next few weeks, and suggested that branches should start attracting local interest in the next competition almost straight away.

Coupons for the new contest will be published fortnightly in The Land from October, 1973 to the end of March, 1974.

Extract from *The Country Woman*, June 1973. Extract courtesy of the CWA.

MADEIRA CAKE

First judged in 1997

Makes: 1 x 20 cm (8 in) round cake

To be cooked in 20 cm round tin. Cake to be approximately 8 cm high.
From Schedule of 1996–97

185 g (6½ oz) butter, softened
2 teaspoons finely grated lemon zest
150 g (5½ oz/⅔ cup) caster sugar
3 eggs
110 g (3¾ oz/¾ cup) plain flour

110 g (3¾ oz/¾ cup) self-raising flour
55 g (2 oz/⅓ cup) mixed peel,
   very finely chopped

1 Preheat oven to 170°C (325°F/Gas 3). Grease a deep 20 cm (8 in) round cake tin and line base with baking paper.

2 Beat butter, lemon zest and sugar in a small bowl until light and fluffy. Add the eggs, one at a time, beating until combined.

3 Transfer mixture to a large bowl, fold in the sifted flours. Spread mixture into the prepared tin, bake for 20 minutes. Sprinkle peel evenly over cake.

4 Bake for about a further 40 minutes or until cooked when tested with a skewer. Stand cake 5 minutes before turning out to cool.

LEMON CAKE

First judged in 1991

Makes: 1 x 20 cm (8 in) round cake

Iced on top only, may be decorated with grated lemon rind or lemon rind cut into fancy shapes.

From Schedule of 1991–92

125 g (4½ oz) butter, softened
150 g (5½ oz/⅔ cup) caster sugar
2 eggs, whisked
125 ml (4 fl oz/½ cup) milk
Finely grated zest of 1½ lemons
185 g (6½ oz/1¼ cups) self-raising flour
Lemon icing, to serve

1   Preheat oven to moderate (180°C/350°F/Gas 4). Grease a 20 cm (8 in) round cake tin and line base with baking paper.

2   Cream butter and sugar. Gradually add whisked eggs, the milk and lemon zest, then fold in sifted flour.

3   Pour into the prepared tin. Bake for 30 minutes or until cooked when tested with a skewer. When cold, ice with lemon icing.

CITRUS SOUR CREAM CAKE

First judged in 2012

Makes: 1 loaf

To be cooked in loaf tin, un-iced, no decoration.
From Schedule of 2011–12

125 g (4½ oz) butter, softened
220 g (7¾ oz/1 cup) caster sugar
3 eggs
75 g (2¾ oz/½ cup) mixed peel
110 g (3¾ oz/¾ cup) self-raising flour

110 g (3¾ oz/¾ cup) plain flour
125 g (4½ oz/½ cup) sour cream

1   Preheat oven to 160°C (315°F/Gas 2–3). Grease a 9 x 19 cm
(3½ x 7½ in) loaf tin and line base with baking paper.

2   Cream butter in a bowl, add sugar and beat until pale and creamy. Whisk
in eggs one at a time, beat well after each addition. Stir in mixed peel.

3   Sift flours together. Stir in half the sifted flours and half the sour cream.
Finally, stir in the remaining flours and sour cream. Spread mixture
into the prepared tin.

4   Bake for about 1–1¼ hours or until cooked. Stand 5 minutes before
turning out to cool on a tea towel-covered rack.

GLUTEN-FREE LEMON TEA CAKE

First judged in 2012

Makes: 1 x 20 cm (8 in) round cake

To be cooked in a 20 cm round tin, un-iced, no decoration.
From Schedule of 2011–12

6 eggs, separated

220 g (7¾ oz/1 cup) caster sugar

2 teaspoons finely grated lemon zest

1 tablespoon lemon juice

200 g (7 oz/2 cups) ground almonds

½ teaspoon almond essence

1 Preheat oven to 160°C (315°F/Gas 2–3). Grease a 20 cm (8 in) round cake tin and line base with baking paper.

2 Whisk the egg yolks, sugar and lemon zest in a small bowl until pale and creamy. Stir in lemon juice, ground almonds and almond essence. Transfer mixture to a larger bowl.

3 Whisk egg whites in a clean, dry bowl until soft peaks form. Gently fold into almond mixture. Pour into the prepared tin. Bake for about 45 minutes or until cooked when tested with a skewer. Turn out onto a tea towel-covered rack to cool.

LIME AND BUTTERMILK CAKE

First judged in 2006

Makes: 1 x 20 cm (8 in) round cake

250 g (9 oz) butter, softened
220 g (7¾ oz/1 cup) caster sugar
1 tablespoon finely grated lime zest
3 eggs, separated

300 g (10½ oz/2 cups) self-raising flour
250 ml (9 fl oz/1 cup) buttermilk
1–2 tablespoons lime juice (optional,
   see tip)

1   Preheat oven to moderate (180°C/350°F/Gas 4). Grease a 20 cm (8 in) round cake tin and line base with baking paper.

2   Cream butter, sugar and lime zest in a small mixing bowl until pale and creamy. Add and beat in egg yolks one at a time until combined. Transfer to a large mixing bowl.

3   Stir in half of the sifted flour, half of the buttermilk and half of the lime juice, if using (see tip), then stir in the balance of the sifted flour, buttermilk and lime juice.

4   Whisk egg whites until soft peaks form. Fold in about half of the whites into mixture then fold in remainder—it will mix in better. Spread into the prepared tin. Bake for about 1 hour or until cooked. Stand for 10 minutes before turning out.

Tip: 1–2 tablespoons of buttermilk can replace the 1–2 tablespoons of lime juice.

AUNT MARY'S

BAKING POWDER

STOP PRESS

Immediately the authorities release additional supplies of essential ingredients, further stocks of AUNT MARY'S BAKING POWDER will be made available throughout Australia.

●There is no substitute for AUNT MARY'S BAKING POWDER, and never will be!

CHOCOLATE BUTTERCAKE

First judged in 1952

Makes: 1 x 18 cm (7 in) round cake

To be iced and may be decorated or piped with a simple design.
May be baked in any shaped deep tin excepting a ring tin.
From Schedule of 1960–61

185 g (6½ oz) butter, softened
3 eggs
165 g (5¾ oz/¾ cup) caster sugar
150 g (5½ oz/1 cup) self-raising flour
75 g (2¾ oz/½ cup) plain flour
40 g (1½ oz/⅓ cup) cocoa powder
125 ml (4 fl oz/½ cup) milk
Chocolate icing, to serve

1   Preheat oven to moderate (180°C/350°F/Gas 4). Grease a deep 18 cm (7 in) round cake tin and line base with baking paper.

2   Combine all ingredients in medium bowl of electric mixer and beat on low speed until ingredients are combined. Increase speed to medium and beat until mixture is smooth and changed in colour.

3   Pour mixture into the prepared tin and bake for about 1 hour until cooked when tested with a skewer. Stand a few minutes before turning out. When cooled, ice with chocolate icing.

CHOCOLATE RIPPLE CAKE

First judged in 2005

Makes: 1 x 20 cm (8 in) round cake

Iced on top only with chocolate icing. No decoration.
From Schedule of 2004–05

125 g (4½ oz) butter, softened
165 g (5¾ oz/¾ cup) sugar
2 eggs
225 g (8 oz/1½ cups) self-raising flour
160 ml (5¼ fl oz/⅔ cup) milk
Chocolate icing, to serve

Ripple mixture

1 tablespoon cocoa powder
55 g (2 oz/¼ cup) sugar
40 g (1½ oz/⅓ cup) chopped walnuts
2 teaspoons butter

1   Preheat oven to moderate (180°C/350°F/Gas 4). Grease a 20 cm (8 in) round cake tin and line base with baking paper.

2   Cream butter and sugar in a bowl, add eggs one at a time and mix well after each addition. Sift flour and add alternately with the milk. Spoon half the mixture into the tin.

3   Combine all the ripple mixture ingredients in a bowl, mixing through the butter. Sprinkle over the cake mixture in the prepared tin. Spread remaining cake mixture on top.

4   Bake for 35 minutes or until cooked when tested with a skewer. When cool, ice the top with chocolate icing.

MARBLE CAKE

First judged in 1977

Makes: 1 x 20 cm (8 in) round cake

220 g (7¾ oz) butter, softened

220 g (7¾ oz/1 cup) caster sugar

1 teaspoon vanilla essence

3 eggs

150 g (5½ oz/1 cup) plain flour,
  well sifted

150 g (5½ oz/1 cup) self-raising
  flour, well sifted

185 ml (6 fl oz/¾ cup) milk,
  at room temperature

Pink food colouring

1 tablespoon cocoa powder

Pale pink icing, to serve

1   Preheat oven to moderate (180°C/350°F/Gas 4). Grease a deep 20 cm
    (8 in) round cake tin and line base with baking paper.

2   Cream butter and sugar very well, add vanilla. Add eggs one at a time,
    beating well after each addition. Fold in the well-sifted flours alternately
    with the milk.

3   Divide the mixture into three equal parts. Leave one part natural, colour
    one pink and use the cocoa mixed with a little hot water to colour the
    chocolate portion. Place alternate spoonfuls of the different mixtures into
    the prepared tin. Lightly tap tin on bench and run a knife through mixture
    four times to give the marble effect.

4   Bake for about 50 minutes. When cold, ice with pale pink icing.

NEAPOLITAN CAKE

First judged in 2009

Makes: 1 x 20 cm (8 in) round cake

To be cooked in 20 cm tin. Pink icing on top.
From Schedule of 2008–09

125 g (4½ oz) butter, softened

220 g (7¾ oz/1 cup) sugar

2 eggs

300 g (10½ oz/2 cups) self-raising flour

Pinch of salt

125 ml (4 fl oz/½ cup) milk

25 g (1 oz/¼ cup) desiccated coconut

Few drops of strawberry essence and
   pink food colouring

6 teaspoons strawberry jam

Pale pink icing, to serve

1   Preheat oven to moderate (180°C/350°F/Gas 4). Grease a 20 cm (8 in) round cake tin and line base with baking paper.

2   Cream butter and sugar until pale and creamy. Add eggs one at a time and beat well. Sift the flour and salt, and stir into the creamed mixture alternately with the milk.

3   Divide mixture into two even portions. To one half, add coconut, to the other half add a few drops of essence and enough pink food colouring to make a pale pink.

4   In the prepared tin, spread white mixture on bottom. Add strawberry jam in drops all over the mixture, and finally pour the pink mixture on top and spread out. Bake for about 45 minutes or until cooked. When cold, ice with pink icing.

Triumphant: Admiring each other's cups after *The Land* Cookery finals at the Town Hall last week are Mrs H. J. Thomas, who received one on behalf of Mrs A. T. Booth, of Bearbong, Mrs Martel, of Dirnaseer and Mrs E. Litchfield, of Leeton, June 1962. Photo courtesy of *The Land*.

RAINBOW CAKE 1

First judged in 1952

Makes: 1 x 20 cm (8 in) round layered cake

Must be put together in the following order: Brown at the base, pink in the centre and cream on top. Layers must be presented as baked—not trimmed. Layers must be joined with a thin layer of buttercream or butter icing. This is to facilitate carrying. Cakes must be simply iced and pipework must not be used.

From Schedule of 1964–65

250 g (9 oz) butter, softened

220 g (7¾ oz/1 cup) caster sugar

Pinch of salt

6 eggs, well whisked

300 g (10½ oz/2 cups) self-raising flour, sifted

250 ml (9 fl oz/1 cup) milk

Lemon essence

Red food colouring

1 tablespoon cocoa powder

1 tablespoon boiling water

Desiccated coconut, to decorate

Buttercream filling

125 g (4½ oz) butter, softened

Up to 185 g (6½ oz/1½ cups) pure icing sugar

½ teaspoon vanilla essence

Warm icing

125 g (4½ oz) butter, chopped

2 teaspoons boiling water

Approximately 500 g (1 lb 2 oz/4 cups) pure icing sugar

1   Preheat oven to moderate (180°C/350°F/Gas 4). Grease three 20 cm (8 in) round cake tins.

2   Cream butter and sugar together, then add salt and well-whisked eggs a bit at a time. Gradually stir in the flour alternately with the milk.

3   Take out approximately one-third of the mixture, put into a bowl and flavour with half a teaspoon of lemon essence. Colour another third pink with red food colouring—it needs to be quite a deep pink. For the chocolate layer add the cocoa, which has been well dissolved in the boiling water. If the mixture looks a little thin add a little extra flour. Put mixtures separately into the three prepared tins and smooth surfaces. Bake for about 20 minutes. Turn onto wire racks to cool.

4   To make the buttercream filling, in an electric mixer, beat butter until fluffy and white. With beaters running, add icing sugar and vanilla. Beat to a spreadable consistency.

5   To make the warm icing, stand a heatproof bowl over barely simmering water; soften butter with boiling water in the bowl. Add enough icing sugar, beating all the while with a wooden spoon until a smooth spreadable consistency.

6   To assemble, place cooled chocolate cake layer at bottom, then pink and then white with buttercream filling between each layer. Ice on top and sides with warm icing. Take coconut and pat it all over the cake while the icing is still warm.

RAINBOW CAKE 2

First judged in 1952

Makes: 1 x 20 cm (8 in) round layered cake

280 g (10 oz) butter or margarine

330 g (11¾ oz/1½ cups) caster sugar

4 large eggs

225 g (8 oz/1½ cups) plain flour

225 g (8 oz/1½ cups) self-raising flour

310 ml (10¾ fl oz/1¼ cups) milk,
   at room temperature

½ teaspoon vanilla essence

Red food colouring

1 tablespoon cocoa powder

Raspberry jam, to serve

White icing, to serve

Desiccated coconut, to serve

1 Preheat oven to moderate (180°C/350°F/Gas 4). Grease and flour three
   20 cm (8 in) round cake tins.

2 Cream butter or margarine at room temperature with the sugar. Add the
   eggs, one at a time, beating after each addition. Sift flours four to five times
   and add to mixture alternately with milk. Add vanilla, mix well.

3 Divide into three equal portions: leave one natural; colour one pink (use a
   few drops of red food colouring—be careful not to overcolour); colour one
   chocolate by mixing the cocoa with a little hot water, blend well and then
   stir into the batter. Spread the mixtures separately into the three prepared
   tins and smooth surface. Bake for about 20 minutes until cooked. Turn out
   onto wire racks to cool.

4 Arrange the chocolate on the bottom. Top with raspberry jam, then add the
   pink layer. Top with raspberry jam and add the white layer. Top with white
   icing and sprinkle with coconut.

RAINBOW CAKE 3

First judged in 1952

Makes: 1 x 20 cm (8 in) round layered cake

225 g (8 oz) butter, softened
385 g (13½ oz/1¾ cups) caster sugar
4 eggs
450 g (1 lb/3 cups) self-raising flour (or 300 g/10½ oz/2 cups self-raising flour and 150 g/5½ oz/1 cup plain flour, well sifted together)

250 ml (9 fl oz/1 cup) milk
Pink food colouring
1½ tablespoons cocoa powder
Raspberry jam, to serve
White icing, to serve
Desiccated coconut, to serve

1   Preheat oven to moderate (180°C/350°F/Gas 4). Grease and flour three 20 cm (8 in) round cake tins.

2   Cream butter and sugar until creamy and the sugar is dissolved. Add the eggs one at a time. Add flour alternately to mixture with milk.

3   Divide into three equal portions: leave one natural; colour one pink with the pink food colouring; use the cocoa in a little hot water to colour one portion chocolate. Spread the mixtures separately into the three prepared tins and smooth the surface. Bake for about 20 minutes or until cooked when tested. Cool on a wire rack.

4   Arrange with the chocolate layer on the bottom, the pink layer in the middle and the white layer on top, sandwiched together with raspberry jam. Ice the top layer with white icing and top with coconut.

The Countrywoman

IN NEW SOUTH WALES

Vol. 1, No. 1.

3D

OCTOBER, 1937.

COFFEE CAKE

First judged in 1990

Makes: 1 x 20 cm (8 in) round or square cake

Must contain coffee in mixture, no nuts allowed. Ice on top only with coffee icing, NO decorations allowed.

Important: In judging, the method of cutting right through the centre of the cake must be observed. Cake should be presented as baked. Not trimmed.

From Schedule of 1989–90

125 g (4½ oz) butter, softened
220 g (7¾ oz/1 cup) sugar
3 eggs
Good tablespoon of coffee essence

225 g (8 oz/1½ cups) self-raising flour
(or plain flour with 1½ teaspoons baking powder)
125 ml (4 fl oz/½ cup) milk
Coffee icing, to serve

1   Preheat oven to moderate (180°C/350°F/Gas 4). Grease a 20 cm (8 in) round or square cake tin and line base and side(s) with baking paper.

2   Cream butter and sugar. Add eggs one at a time and beat well after each addition. Add coffee essence, then sift flour and add to mixture in batches, alternating with milk.

3   Pour into the prepared tin. Bake for 35–40 minutes or until cooked when tested. Ice with coffee icing when cooled.

GINGER CAKE

First judged in 1987

Makes: 1 x 20 cm (8 in) round or square cake

125 g (4½ oz) butter, softened

75 g (2¾ oz/⅓ cup) caster sugar

1 egg

260 g (9¼ oz/¾ cup) golden syrup

260 g (9¼ oz/1¾ cups) plain flour

2 teaspoons ground ginger

1 teaspoon ground cinnamon

½ teaspoon bicarbonate of soda

185 ml (6 fl oz/¾ cup) hot water

1   Preheat oven to moderate (180°C/350°F/Gas 4). Grease a deep 20 cm (8 in) round or square cake tin and line base with baking paper.

2   Cream butter and sugar in a small bowl until light and fluffy, add egg and beat until combined. Gradually add golden syrup and beat well.

3   Transfer mixture to a large bowl, stir in half the sifted dry ingredients with half the hot water, then add the remaining sifted dry ingredients and water, stir until smooth.

4   Pour into the prepared tin and bake for about 1 hour until cooked when tested with a skewer. Stand for 10 minutes before turning out. Leave un-iced.

Champion Sponge Maker

Mr H. V. Budd presents the trophy to Mrs J. Chamberlain of Mulgoa. Mrs Malcolm (retiring State Hon. Treasurer) offers her congratulations, June 1959. Photo courtesy of *The Land*.

Where there's an AGA
....there's a happy housewife...

and a Happy .. .. Husband too !

For AGA cooked meals have the true, inimitable flavour of faultlessly cooked food in every delicious bite. Succulent juices and health-giving vitamins are retained. Joints roasted in an AGA have a true roast flavour because their natural juices are sealed inside. An AGA Cooker makes food preparation a pleasure—no basting or turning of joints—no waiting for a hot oven—no watching—no hot stove headaches.

IDEAL FOR CITY OR COUNTRY

Ideal for either city or country, the AGA is continuously alight day and night. Yet its economy is amazing—one scuttle of coke lasts a whole day. Model C (illustrated) is guaranteed not to burn more than £3 worth of coke a year (with coke at 30/- a ton). Larger models, of course, burn more.

Because it is scientifically designed for perfect cooking, an AGA enables you to enjoy unexampled convenience, comfort and economy in food preparation. AGA-owners have found it to be the cleanest, most economical, most efficient, and leisure-giving cooker to be had.

The automatic thermostat ensures accurate temperature control—banishes guess-work —releases the exact amount of heat required to bake, boil, braise, fry, grill, toast, stew, steam, roast and simmer. Meals can be kept at serving temperatures almost indefinitely (even overnight) without impairing their luscious goodness.

No danger of personal injury, no chance of fire. All surfaces are cool, except the hot-plates. Children are safe in an AGA kitchen, for the AGA is thoroughly insulated.

The AGA Cooker is made entirely in Great Britain. Built to last a lifetime, it is guaranteed for 20 years against faulty workmanship and material.

Investigate! You'll be thrilled and delighted by the amazing performance—its low-cost operation. Call at our showrooms for a demonstration, or if more convenient, write for illustrated AGA Booklet J4.

AGA COOKER

LEVIN & CO. LTD. (Inc. in N.Z.),

45 King Street, Sydney, and 432 Bourke Street, Melbourne. S.A. Agents: COLTON, PALMER and PRESTON LTD., Adelaide.

SPEEDWAY CAKE

First judged in 1985

Makes: 1 x 18 cm (7 in) round or square cake

*Competitors 12 years and under.
Even texture, well flavoured and evenly baked in a 7 inch cake tin.
Plain white icing on top. Piping allowed.
From Schedule of 1984–85*

115 g (4 oz) butter, softened

¾ breakfast cup sugar

2 eggs

1 breakfast cup self-raising flour

60 ml (2 fl oz/¼ cup) milk

Finely grated zest of 1 orange

Pinch of salt

1   Preheat oven to moderate (180°C/350°F/Gas 4). Grease an 18 cm (7 in) round or square cake tin and line base with baking paper.

2   Put everything into a basin and beat hard for 5 minutes or until the mixture looks creamy and spongy.

3   Pour into the prepared tin. Bake for 30–45 minutes. Best eaten day it is made.

MOIST COCONUT CAKE

First judged in 1986

Makes: 1 x 20 cm (8 in) round cake

To be iced on top only and dusted with coconut. Approximate 6 cm depth desired.
To be cooked in 20 cm round tin.

From Schedule of 1985–86

125 g (4½ oz) butter, softened

220 g (7¾ oz/1 cup) caster sugar

½ teaspoon coconut essence

2 eggs

45 g (1¾ oz/½ cup) desiccated coconut

225 g (8 oz/1½ cups) self-raising
  flour, sifted

300 g (10½ oz) sour cream

80 ml (2½ fl oz/⅓ cup) milk

Frosting

250 g (9 oz/2 cups) icing sugar

2 egg whites, lightly whisked

120 g (4¼ oz/1⅓ cups) desiccated
  coconut

Pink food colouring

1   Preheat oven to moderate (180°C/350°F/Gas 4). Grease a 20 cm (8 in) round cake tin and line base with baking paper.

2   Cream butter and sugar, add coconut essence, then beat in eggs one at a time, combining well. Stir in half the desiccated coconut and sifted flour with half the sour cream and milk, then stir in remaining ingredients.

3   Put in the prepared tin and smooth the surface. Bake for about 1 hour until cooked when tested with a skewer. Cool on a wire rack.

4   To make frosting, combine sifted icing sugar with egg whites. Mix well, add coconut and a little colouring. Spread over top of cooled cake.

HONEY COCONUT CAKE

First judged in 2008

Makes: 1 x 20 cm (8 in) round cake

45 g (1¾ oz/½ cup) desiccated coconut
125 g (4½ oz) butter, softened
165 g (5¾ oz/¾ cup, firmly packed)
  brown sugar
2 eggs
2 tablespoons honey
225 g (8 oz/1½ cup) self-raising flour
125 ml (4 fl oz/½ cup) milk

Caramel icing

30 g (1 oz) butter
110 g (3¾ oz/½ cup, firmly packed)
  brown sugar
2 tablespoons milk
125–185 g (4½–6½ oz/1–1½ cups)
  icing sugar

1   Preheat oven to moderate (180°C/350°F/Gas 4). Grease a 20 cm (8 in) round cake tin and line base with baking paper. Place the coconut in a heavy-based frying pan over low heat and allow to brown evenly. Remove and cool.

2   Cream the butter and sugar in a small bowl till pale and creamy, add eggs one at a time, then add honey, beat until combined. Transfer to a large bowl, fold in toasted coconut, half the sifted flour and half the milk, then remaining flour and milk.

3   Spread into the prepared tin. Bake for 40–50 minutes or until cooked when tested. Cool on a wire rack.

4   To make the icing, melt butter, brown sugar and milk in a saucepan, stir constantly over heat until mixture boils. Turn down heat, simmer 3 minutes without stirring. Stir in enough sifted icing sugar to form a firm spreading consistency. Spread evenly over cooled cake while warm.

GINGER BUTTERCAKE

First judged in 1987

Makes: 1 x 18 cm (7 in) round cake or 1 loaf

Lemon icing on top only, piping decorations allowed.
From Schedule of 1986–87

125 g (4½ oz) butter, softened
110 g (3¾ oz/½ cup) sugar
175 g (6 oz/½ cup) golden syrup
2 eggs
225 g (8 oz/1½ cups) plain flour

2 teaspoons ground ginger
1 teaspoon ground cinnamon
1 teaspoon bicarbonate of soda
60 ml (2 fl oz/¼ cup) boiling water

1   Preheat oven to moderate (180°C/350°F/Gas 4). Grease an 18 cm (7 in) round cake tin or 9 x 19 cm (3½ x 7½ in) loaf tin and line base with baking paper.

2   Beat butter and sugar in a bowl until pale and creamy, then beat in golden syrup, add eggs one at a time. Sift together the flour and spices. Fold in the dry ingredients. Lastly add bicarbonate of soda, dissolved in the water.

3   Pour into the prepared tin and bake for 45 minutes. Turn out onto a wire rack to cool.

ORIENTAL GINGERBREAD

First judged in 1976

Makes: 1 x 20 cm (8 in) square cake

125 g (4½ oz) butter, softened

55 g (2 oz/¼ cup) sugar

2 eggs

1 tablespoon golden syrup

300 g (10½ oz/2 cups) self-raising flour

1 teaspoon ground cinnamon

1 teaspoon ground ginger

3 tablespoons desiccated coconut

125–185 ml (4–6 fl oz/½–¾ cup)
warm water

35 g (1¼ oz/½ cup) shredded coconut,
lightly toasted, to decorate

Icing

185 g (6½ oz/1½ cups) icing sugar

2 teaspoons butter, softened

1 teaspoon coffee essence

Hot water

1 Preheat oven to moderate (180°C/350°F/Gas 4). Grease a 20 cm (8 in) square cake tin and line base with baking paper.

2 Beat butter and sugar to a cream. Add eggs one at a time, then beat in the golden syrup. Sift together the flour and spices and fold into the batter, then sprinkle in the desiccated coconut.

3 Add enough warm water to mix to a smooth consistency and thoroughly beat the mixture. Pour into the prepared tin. Bake for 45 minutes.

4 For the icing, beat all ingredients together, using enough hot water to mix to a spreading consistency. Spread over cooled cake then sprinkle with the shredded coconut.

Competitors making sponge cakes at Sydney City Council Electricity Showrooms, June 1956.
Photo courtesy of *The Land*.

JAZZ CAKE

First judged in 1990

Makes: 1 x 18 cm (7 in) round cake

4 tablespoons butter, softened
220 g (7¾ oz/1 cup) sugar
3 eggs, whisked
1 teaspoon vanilla essence
125 ml (4 fl oz/½ cup) milk
185 g (6 fl oz/1¼ cups) plain flour
1 heaped teaspoon baking powder

Pinch of salt
Pink food colouring
2 teaspoons cocoa mixed with
  a little hot water
10–12 dates
5–6 walnuts
Pale pink icing, to serve

1 Preheat oven to moderate (180°C/350°F/Gas 4). Grease an 18 cm (7 in) round cake tin and line base with baking paper.

2 Cream butter and sugar. Gradually add eggs and vanilla and beat well. Then add the milk, alternately with the sifted flour, baking powder and salt.

3 Divide the mixture into three parts: colour one pink with the pink food colouring, one with the cocoa mixture to colour the chocolate portion and leave one as is.

4 Prepare dates by splitting them lengthways and inserting half a walnut into each. Arrange dates over the base of the prepared tin and add mixture as for a marble cake (place alternate spoonfuls of the different mixtures into the tin). Bake for 35–40 minutes or until cooked. Ice with pale pink icing when cold.

AMY JOHNSON CAKE

First judged in 2011

Makes: 1 x 20 cm (8 in) square cake

To be cooked in a 20 cm square tin. Lemon icing.
From Schedule of 2010–11

*Lemon icing and desiccated coconut,
to decorate*

115 g (4 oz/⅓ cup) raspberry jam
140 g (5 oz/1 cup) currants

Base

150 g (5½ oz/1 cup) self-raising flour
Pinch of salt
60 g (2¼ oz) butter, softened
A little milk

Topping

2 eggs
165 g (5¾ oz/¾ cup) sugar
150 g (5½ oz/1 cup) self-raising flour
2 tablespoons melted butter
60 ml (2 fl oz/¼ cup) milk

1 Preheat oven to moderate (180°C/350°F/Gas 4). Grease a 20 cm (8 in) square cake tin and line base with baking paper. Sift flour and salt into a bowl and rub in the butter. Mix to a firm dough with a little milk.

2 Roll out to 6 mm (¼ in) thickness and cover the base of the tin with the pastry. Spread with raspberry jam and sprinkle with currants.

3 For the topping, whisk eggs and sugar in a bowl until light and fluffy. Fold in sifted flour and finally the melted butter and milk. Pour on top of pastry.

4 Bake for about 40 minutes or until cooked and golden brown. When cold, ice with lemon icing and sprinkle with coconut.

BUTTERSCOTCH CAKE

First judged in 2011

Makes: 1 x 20 cm (8 in) round cake

To be cooked in 20 cm tin. Caramel icing on top.
From Schedule of 2010–11

250 g (9 oz) butter, softened

1 teaspoon vanilla essence

185 g (6½ oz/1 cup, lightly packed)
  dark brown sugar

2 eggs, separated

1 tablespoon golden syrup

150 g (5½ oz/1 cup) self-raising flour

75 g (2¾ oz/½ cup) plain flour

½ teaspoon ground cinnamon

125 ml (4 fl oz/½ cup) milk

Pinch of salt

Caramel icing

60 g (2¼ oz) butter

110 g (3¾ oz/½ cup, firmly packed)
  dark brown sugar

60 ml (2 fl oz/¼ cup) milk

90–125 g (3¼–4½ oz/¾–1 cup)
  icing sugar

1 Preheat oven to moderate (180°C/350°F/Gas 4). Grease a deep 20 cm (8 in) round cake tin and line base with baking paper.

2 Cream butter with the vanilla; add the sugar and beat until pale and creamy. Whisk in egg yolks and golden syrup, beat until well combined.

3 Fold in sifted flours and cinnamon alternately with milk. Whisk egg whites with salt until soft peaks form, fold gently into mixture. Spread mixture into the prepared tin. Bake for 50–60 minutes or until cooked when tested with a skewer. Allow to stand for 10 minutes, then turn out the cake onto a folded cloth.

Winning smiles: Cup winners Mrs P. Hammon (Nepean), fancy biscuits; Mrs G. Peck (Nepean), citrus jam; and Mrs G. Devenish (Central West), berry fruit jam, smile their thanks on receiving their championship trophies. Mrs Devenish has won 111 first prizes in Branch, Group and State awards since the inception of the Cookery Competition, June 1961. Photo courtesy of *The Land*.

4   To make the caramel icing, melt butter in a saucepan, add brown sugar and stir over heat for 3 minutes. Gradually add milk, and, stirring, bring to the boil. Remove from heat and leave to cool. When cold, gradually add icing sugar and beat until smooth and spreadable. Spread over the cooled cake.

Home Baking Saves Money

Martha Cromwell explains why it's important to be particular about the ingredients you buy.

THERE'S something very satisfying about making your own cakes. And what woman hasn't blushed prettily and been proud to say, "Oh—I just whipped it up th:s morning . . . quite a simple recipe, really. Why, of course . . .! I'll jot it down for you . . ."

But there's another thing about home baking which is very important indeed: even with the present cost of ingredients, **it's much more economical**—but only if you choose ingredients which ensure against failures.

The loveliest fruit in Nature's basket, the luscious grape, produces the finest and highest quality rising ingredient yet known to the science of cooking: pure Cream of Tartar.

You might ask: "Why be so particular about using **Cream of Tartar** as a rising ingredient?"

A number of cookery experts, in England as Australia, and food chemists have applied various tests and agree that Cream of Tartar is still the best rising ingredient. They say that Cream of Tartar should be preferred to any of its substitutes.

Extract from *The Country Woman*, June 1953. Extract courtesy of the CWA.

BANANA CAKE

First judged in 1975

Makes: 1 loaf

To be iced on TOP only. Approximately 2½ inch minimum depth of cake is desirable.
From Schedule of 1974–75

125 g (4½ oz) butter, softened

125 g (4½ oz/⅔ cup, lightly packed) brown sugar

2 eggs

250 g (9 oz/1⅔ cups) self-raising flour

Pinch of salt

1 teaspoon bicarbonate of soda

60 ml (2 fl oz/¼ cup) milk

1½ ripe bananas

2 teaspoons lemon juice

Lemon icing, to serve

1 Preheat oven to moderate (180°C/350°F/Gas 4). Grease a 9 x 19 cm (3½ x 7½ in) loaf tin and line base with baking paper.

2 Cream butter and sugar, add eggs, then beat well. Sift the flour and salt together three times. Dissolve bicarbonate of soda in the milk. Mash bananas, add lemon juice and stir into the creamed mixture. Fold the flour and milk alternately into cake mixture.

3 Place into the prepared tin and bake for 45 minutes (or until cooked). When cool, ice with lemon icing.

PEACH BLOSSOM CAKE 1

First judged in 1983

Makes: 1 x 20 cm (8 in) round cake

125 g (4½ oz) butter, softened
220 g (7¾ oz/1 cup) sugar
4 egg whites
125 ml (4 fl oz/½ cup) milk
225 g (8 oz/1½ cups) plain flour
1 heaped teaspoon baking powder
Pink food colouring
Pale pink icing, to serve

1   Preheat oven to moderate (180°C/350°F/Gas 4). Grease a 20 cm (8 in)
    round cake tin and line base with baking paper.

2   Cream the butter and sugar. Stiffly whisk the egg whites in a separate bowl.
    Fold in the egg white, then slowly fold in milk and lastly add the sifted flour
    and baking powder.

3   Divide mixture into two, colour one half pale pink, arrange small spoonfuls
    of the two batters into the prepared tin and bake for 30–40 minutes. Ice on
    top only with pale pink icing.

PEACH BLOSSOM CAKE 2

First judged in 1983

Makes: 1 x 20 cm (8 in) round cake

185 g (6½ oz) butter, softened
330 g (11¾ oz/1½ cups) caster sugar
6 egg whites
225 g (8 oz/1½ cups) plain flour
90 g (3¼ oz/¾ cup) cornflour

1½ teaspoons baking powder
125 ml (4 fl oz/½ cup) milk,
    at room temperature
Pink food colouring
Pale pink icing, to serve

1 Preheat oven to moderate (180°C/350°F/Gas 4). Grease a 20 cm (8 in) round cake tin and line base with baking paper.

2 Cream the butter and sugar well. Fold in the stiffly whisked egg whites followed by the combined and sifted flour, cornflour and baking powder, and lastly fold through the milk. Divide mixture into two and colour one half a soft pink.

3 Place in the prepared tin as for a marble cake (do not marble) to give the effect of peach blossom. (Place 1 spoonful pink, 1 spoonful white, then white on pink, pink on white.) Bake for 1–1¼ hours or until cooked when tested with a skewer. Cool on a wire rack. Ice on top with pale pink icing.

SPONGE SANDWICH

First judged in 1956

Makes: 1 x sandwiched 18 cm (7 in) round cake

Points to be looked for in judging: The cake should be smooth and even in appearance and well and evenly risen. Both layers should be even thickness. It should be golden brown in colour both on top and sides. There should be a close, fine texture, light in proportion to size and showing no holes or cracks in the surface. The crust should not be tough or coarse and the mixture should not be moist or sticky. The cake should be elastic to touch and not showing too much shrinking in baking.

From Schedule of 1964–65

3 eggs

110 g (3¾ oz/½ cup) sugar

110 g (3¾ oz/¾ cup) plain flour

½ teaspoon cream of tartar (see tip)

¼ teaspoon bicarbonate of soda (see tip)

60 ml (2 fl oz/¼ cup) water

1 teaspoon butter

Raspberry or apricot jam, to serve

1   Preheat oven to moderate (180°C/350°F/Gas 4). Grease and flour two 18 cm (7 in) round cake tins. Separate egg whites from yolks. Whisk whites stiffly, add yolks, then sugar, whisking until mixture is stiff and thick. Stir in well the sifted flour, cream of tartar and bicarbonate of soda. Boil water and butter, pour on to cake mixture, and stir lightly but thoroughly.

2   Pour into the prepared tins and bake for 15–20 minutes. Turn out onto wire racks to cool. Join layers together with raspberry or apricot jam.

Tip: You can replace the cream of tartar and bicarbonate of soda with 1 teaspoon baking powder.

Mrs E. Lindbeck (Dirnaseer Branch), Champion Spongemaker in *The Land* Cookery Finals, 1956. Photo courtesy of *The Land*.

CORNFLOUR SPONGE SANDWICH

First judged in 1987

Makes: 1 x sandwiched 20 cm (8 in) sponge cake

Jam filled. A four-egg recipe to be used.
From Schedule of 2000–01

125 g (4½ oz/1 cup) cornflour

1 teaspoon cream of tartar

½ teaspoon bicarbonate of soda

Pinch of salt

4 eggs

110 g (3¾ oz/½ cup) caster sugar

1 teaspoon vanilla essence

Approximately 115 g (4 oz/⅓ cup)
    raspberry jam

1 Preheat oven to moderate (180°C/350°F/Gas 4). Grease two deep 20 cm (8 in) sponge tins, dust with flour. Sift the cornflour, cream of tartar, bicarbonate of soda and salt three times.

2 Whisk eggs, sugar and vanilla together for 10 minutes. Fold in sifted ingredients.

3 Divide mixture evenly between the prepared tins. Bake for 15 minutes. Turn out onto a clean tea towel. When cold, join together with raspberry jam.

CHOCOLATE SPONGE 1

First judged in 1998

Makes: 1 x sandwiched 18 cm (7 in) round cake

Fresh cream filled. No cornflour. A four-egg recipe to be used.

Hints to the competitor: Layers to be evenly risen, identical in thickness and baking. Tops should be smooth and without sugar spots. Texture should be fine, creamy, delicate and spongy when lightly pressed with the fingertips. Cooler rack marks must not show on cakes. Leave un-iced. No icing sugar or dusting allowed on top of sponge. To be cooked in two 18 cm or 7 inch round cake tins. Group finalist to be sent to State Finals 1998 Unfilled. If first prize winner unable to compete in finals, the second placegetter may be nominated.

From Schedule of 1997–98

4 eggs, separated

165 g (5¾ oz/¾ cup) caster sugar

150 g (5½ oz/1 cup) plain flour

1 teaspoon bicarbonate of soda

¼ teaspoon salt

1 teaspoon cream of tartar

2 tablespoons cocoa powder

1 tablespoon butter

2 teaspoons golden syrup

80 ml (2½ fl oz/⅓ cup) hot water

Jam and whipped cream, to serve

1   Preheat oven to moderate (180°C/350°F/Gas 4). Grease two 18 cm (7 in) round cake tins and line bases with baking paper. Whisk the egg whites in a bowl until stiff, add the sugar gradually, whisk until thick, add egg yolks and whisk 3 minutes.

2   Sift dry ingredients, fold into the mixture. Blend butter, golden syrup and the water together. Stir carefully into mixture. Spoon mixture evenly into the prepared tins, bake for 20–25 minutes or until firm to touch. Cool on a wire rack. Fill with jam and cream.

CHOCOLATE SPONGE 2

First judged in 1998

Makes: 1 x sandwiched 18 cm (7 in) round cake

1 tablespoon butter

2 tablespoons cocoa powder

2 tablespoons boiling water

4 eggs

165 g (5¾ oz/¾ cup) sugar

150 g (5½ oz/1 cup) self-raising flour

Jam and whipped cream, to serve

1   Preheat oven to moderate (180°C/350°F/Gas 4). Grease two 18 cm (7 in) round cake tins and line bases with baking paper. Melt the butter, add cocoa and mix. Stir in boiling water and put aside to cool.

2   Whisk the eggs and sugar together in a bowl until pale and creamy, about 10 minutes. Gently fold in sifted flour and lastly fold in the cocoa mixture.

3   Divide mixture equally between the prepared tins. Bake for 20 minutes or until firm to the touch. Cool on a wire rack and fill with jam and cream.

CINNAMON SPONGE SANDWICH

First judged in 1993

Makes: 1 x sandwiched 20 cm (8 in) round cake

A four-egg recipe to be used. No cornflour.

Hints to the competitor: Layers to be evenly risen, identical in thickness and baking. Tops should be smooth and without sugar spots. Texture should be fine, creamy, delicate and spongy when lightly pressed with fingertips. Cream to be even and not too thick. Cooler rack marks must not show on cakes. Leave un-iced. No icing sugar or dusting allowed on top of sponge.

From Schedule of 1992–93

4 eggs

220 g (7¾ oz/1 cup) caster sugar

150 g (5½ oz/1 cup) plain flour

2 teaspoons ground cinnamon

2 teaspoons cocoa powder

1 teaspoon baking powder

125 ml (4 fl oz/½ cup) boiling milk

30 g (1 oz) butter

Jam and whipped cream, to serve

1   Preheat oven to moderate (180°C/350°F/Gas 4). Grease and flour two deep 20 cm (8 in) round cake tins.

2   Whisk eggs and sugar for 15 minutes until pale and creamy. Fold in combined and sifted flour, cinnamon, cocoa and baking powder. Add boiling milk in which butter has been melted (see it is boiling fast and frothy). Mix very lightly, pour into the prepared tins.

3   Bake for 20 minutes—take out when cooked—everyone's oven is different so use your own judgment on when the cake is cooked. Turn out to a wire rack to cool. Fill with jam and cream.

Competing in State Championships: Spongemakers at work in County Council Showrooms. Mrs G. Noble, the winner, is in foreground, June 1960. Photo courtesy of *The Land*.

GINGER SPONGE

First judged in 2008

Makes: 1 x sandwiched 18 cm (7 in) round cake

150 g (5½ oz/1 cup) plain flour

1 teaspoon baking powder

2 teaspoons ground ginger

1 teaspoon ground cinnamon

2 teaspoons cocoa powder

4 eggs

55 g (2 oz/¼ cup) caster sugar

Pinch of salt

80 ml (2½ fl oz/⅓ cup) boiling water

1 teaspoon butter

Raspberry jam, to serve

1   Preheat oven to moderate (180°C/350°F/Gas 4). Grease two deep 18 cm (7 in) round sponge tins. Lightly dust with flour. Sift flour, baking powder, spices and cocoa three times to mix.

2   Whisk eggs, sugar and salt in large bowl for 5 minutes until pale and creamy. Sift dry ingredients in batches, on top of mixture. Fold in carefully, using an egg whisk, then fold in the boiling water containing the butter. Mix lightly.

3   Divide mixture evenly between the prepared tins. Bake for 20–25 minutes. Turn out onto a clean tea towel. When cool, join together with jam.

"The Land" Cookery Contest Winners

Dark Fruit Cake: Mrs. C. Tongue (Nundle), Mrs. A. McManus (Mudgee), Mrs. A. Gault (Trundle).

Sultana Cake: Mrs. Caldwell (Wallendbeen), Mrs. R. McKenzie (Molong), Mrs. C. Wiedeman (Inverell).

Orange Cake: Mrs. T. Fenton (Coff's Harbour), Mrs. J. Martel· (Dirnaseer), Mrs. W. England (Penrith).

Chocolate Cake: Mrs. Walker (Mangrove Mt.), Miss J. Plumb (Bega), Mrs. A. McManus (Mudgee).

Rainbow Cake: Miss F. Queen (Canterbury-Bankstown), Mrs. Barrow (Wamberal), Mrs. E. Coffee (Talbragar).

Sponge Sandwich: Mrs. L. Knight (Whitton), Miss L. Leeson (Coraki).

Plain Biscuits: Mrs. J. Bennett (Wallendbeen), Mrs. F. Godwin (Henty), Mrs. Chamney (Canowindra).

Highly commended special prize to Miss D. Baker (Gunnedah).

Fancy Biscuits: Mrs. Morrow (Grafton), Mrs. G. Hammon (Leura), Mrs. C. N. Baker (Gunnedah).

Sweets: Mrs. Cook (Long Jetty), Mrs. R. Hancock (Ingleburn), Mrs. G. Hammon (Leura).

Stone Fruit Jam: Mrs. R. McKay (Belgravia), Mrs. Rheinberger (Meroo), Miss M. Hall (Coolabah).

Citrus Jam: Mrs. E. C. Hannigan (Broken Hill), Mrs. Floyd (Wamberal), Mrs. C. Wholohan (Penrith).

Any Other Jam: Mrs. G. A. Devenish (Neville), Mrs. Buckmaster (Canberra), Mrs. F. Godwin (Henty).

Special Occasion Cake: Mrs. Jones (Eastwood-Epping), Mrs. Evans (St. George), Mrs. H. G. Templeton (Leeton).

Novelty Cake: Mrs. C. N. Baker (Gunnedah), Miss J. Bourchier (Blighty), Mrs. R. J. Lamrock (Inverell).

Decorated Iced Cake: Mrs. C. N. Baker (Gunnedah), Mrs. L. Hanson (Batlow), Miss E. Trefford (Canowindra).

Boiled Plum Pudding: Mrs. Rawson (Bogan Gate), Mrs. B. M. Wright (Jamberoo), Mrs. J. J. Ryan (Yass).

Extract from *The Country Woman*, July 1963.
Extract courtesy of the CWA.

SWISS ROLL

First judged in 1987

Makes: 1 Swiss roll

Roll must have three turns. Jam-filled only. Ends not to be cut.
Roll should be a honey colour.

From Schedule of 1985–86

5 *eggs*
5 *tablespoons caster sugar*
A little vanilla essence
5 *tablespoons plain flour*
1 *teaspoon baking powder*
Approximately 115 g (4 oz/⅓ cup) jam

1   Preheat oven to 220°C (425°F/Gas 7). Grease a 25 x 30 cm (10 x 12 in) Swiss roll tin. Separate the eggs and whisk the whites until stiff peaks form. Add the yolks and sugar and whisk until stiff. Add a little vanilla, to flavour, and mix well.

2   Sift together flour and baking powder and fold into the egg mixture.

3   Spread evenly into the prepared tin and bake for 10–15 minutes until firm and golden brown. Turn out onto a dry tea towel and roll up quickly lengthways into a log. Allow to cool, then unroll, spread with jam, and re-roll as before.

CHOCOLATE HONEY SPONGE ROLL

First judged in 2012

Makes: 1 sponge roll

3 eggs

150 g (5½ oz) sugar

100 g (3½ oz/⅔ cup) plain flour

1 teaspoon cream of tartar

½ teaspoon bicarbonate of soda

½ teaspoon ground cinnamon

1 tablespoon cocoa powder

80 ml (2½ fl oz/⅓ cup) boiling water

1 teaspoon honey

Mock cream

4 tablespoons caster sugar

80 ml (2½ fl oz/⅓ cup) water

125 g (4½ oz) butter, softened

1 teaspoon vanilla essence

1   Preheat oven to moderate (180°C/350°F/Gas 4). Grease a 25 x 30 cm (10 x 12 in) Swiss roll tin and line base with baking paper.

2   Whisk eggs and sugar in a bowl until pale and creamy. Sift together the dry ingredients (except the cocoa) then gently fold into the creamed mixture. Dissolve the cocoa in the boiling water and then gently fold into the mixture with the honey. Spread into the prepared tin. Bake for about 12 minutes. When cooked, immediately roll lengthways in a tea towel, leaving roll to cool.

3   To make the mock cream, dissolve the sugar in the water in a small saucepan and bring to the boil. Then cool. Cream the butter, then gradually beat in the cooled water and sugar mixture and the vanilla.

4   Gently unroll the cooled sponge, fill with the mock cream and re-roll 1–1½ turns. Do not trim the ends and do not sprinkle with sugar.

PATTY CAKES

First judged in 1992

Makes: about 20 patty cakes

To be cooked in patty tins NOT patty papers. Iced and decorated.
From Schedule of 1991–92

125 g (4½ oz) butter, softened
165 g (5¾ oz/¾ cup) sugar
150 g (5½ oz/1 cup) self-raising flour
2 eggs
60 ml (2 fl oz/¼ cup) milk
¼ teaspoon vanilla essence
Pink or white glacé icing, to serve

1   Preheat oven to moderate (180°C/350°F/Gas 4). Grease the patty tins.
    Put everything (except the icing) into a mixing bowl and beat hard for
    5 minutes or until the mixture looks pale and creamy.

2   Spoon evenly into the patty tins (not paper cases). Bake for 10–15 minutes.

3   When cooled, remove from patty tins and ice with pink or white glacé
    icing.

SEED CAKE

First judged in 1988

Makes: 1 x 20 cm (8 in) round cake

Un-iced.
From Schedule of 1987–88

125 g (4½ oz) butter, softened
165 g (5¾ oz/¾ cup) sugar
Pinch of salt
2 eggs

125 ml (4 fl oz/½ cup) milk
1 tablespoon caraway seeds
300 g (10½ oz/2 cups) plain flour
3 teaspoons baking powder

1 Preheat oven to 200°C (400°F/Gas 6). Grease a 20 cm (8 in) round cake tin and line base with baking paper.

2 Cream butter, sugar and salt in a bowl then whisk the eggs well and add gradually to the mixture. Beat in the milk and caraway seeds.

3 Sift the flour and baking powder together then mix lightly into the mixture. Pour into the prepared tin. Bake for 1–1¼ hours. Cool on a wire rack.

LAMINGTONS 1

First judged in 1965

Makes: twenty-five 3 cm (1¼ in) squares

Eight cakes must be presented. The base must be a buttercake with no jam filling.
From Schedule of 1964–65

90 g (3¼ oz) butter, softened

75 g (2¾ oz/⅓ cup) caster sugar

2 eggs

110 g (3¾ oz/¾ cup) plain flour,
  plus extra

1 teaspoon baking powder

Pinch of salt

1 tablespoon milk

1½ tablespoons melted butter

Dark chocolate icing, of thin spreading
  thickness, to coat

Desiccated coconut, to decorate

1   Preheat oven to moderate (180°C/350°F/Gas 4). Grease a 15 cm
    (6 in) square sandwich tin and line base with baking paper. Beat butter
    with wooden spoon first, adding in the sugar. Then beat with electric mixer
    until pale and creamy, add 2 eggs, one at a time, and add a little
    of measured flour if curdling.

2   Sift flour with the baking powder and a little salt. Gradually add milk
    alternately with flour. Fold in the melted butter last. Pour into the prepared
    tin. Bake for 30 minutes. This cake should come from the tin flat on top
    and need very little trimming.

3   Cut when cold into 3 cm (1¼ in) pieces. Dip into the dark chocolate icing
    to coat lightly and then finish with the coconut.

Tip: Vanilla added to icing brings out the chocolate flavour.

Photo from *The Land* 1966–67 Cookery Contest Schedule. Photo courtesy of the CWA.

LAMINGTONS 2

First judged in 1965

Makes: 12 squares

90 g (3¼ oz) butter, softened
110 g (3¾ oz/½ cup) caster sugar
2 eggs
150 g (5½ oz/1 cup) plain flour
1 teaspoon baking powder

Pinch of salt
1½ tablespoons milk
Thin chocolate icing, to coat
Desiccated coconut, to decorate

1 Preheat oven to 170°C (325°F/Gas 3). Grease a 4 x 15 cm (1½ x 6 in) square slab tin and line base with baking paper.

2 Cream butter and sugar together. Beat in eggs, one at a time. Sift flour with the baking powder and salt, then add to the mixture in batches, alternating with the milk. Pour into the prepared tin and smooth the surface.

3 Bake for 25–30 minutes or until cooked. Cool on a wire rack, then cut into required size. Cover with chocolate icing then roll in fine coconut.

Tip: The lamington cake is best made the day before coating with icing and decorating with coconut.

CHERRY CAKE 1

First judged in 1975

Makes: 1 x 18 cm (7 in) round cake

Cherries should be well drained of syrup, left whole or cut in halves or quarters only. Use plain flour and baking powder for a better base. Approximately 2½ inch depth of cake is desirable. Iced with a simple icing only, no decorations.

From Schedule of 1974–75

125 g (4½ oz) butter, softened

110 g (3¾ oz/½ cup) caster sugar

1 teaspoon vanilla essence

2 eggs

90 g (3¼ oz) glacé cherries, tinned or
   bottled, washed and dried of syrup

110 g (3¾ oz/¾ cup) plain flour

110 g (3¾ oz/¾ cup) self-raising flour

60 ml (2 fl oz/¼ cup) milk,
   at room temperature

White glacé icing, tinted pale pink
   (optional), to serve

1   Preheat oven to 160°C (315°F/Gas 2–3). Grease an 18 cm (7 in) round cake tin and line base with baking paper.

2   Cream butter, sugar and vanilla well. Beat in eggs one at a time. Add cherries which have been dusted with a little of the measured flour.

3   Sift the flours four times and add alternately with milk. Mix well. Bake for about 1 hour or until cooked. Cool in tin then ice with glacé icing, if liked.

CHERRY CAKE 2

First judged in 1975

Makes: 1 x 18 cm (7 in) round cake

125 g (4½ oz) butter, softened

Vanilla essence, to taste

165 g (5¾ oz/¾ cup) sugar

2 large eggs

3 tablespoons chopped glacé cherries

225 g (8 oz/1½ cups) self-raising flour,
 sifted

100 ml (3½ fl oz) water

White glacé icing, to serve

Extra glacé cherries, to decorate

1 Preheat oven to 170°C (325°F/Gas 3). Grease an 18 cm (7 in) round cake tin and line base with baking paper.

2 Beat the butter and vanilla, add sugar and cream well. Whisk the eggs and gradually add to creamed mixture, beating well. Stir in cherries.

3 Fold in the sifted flour alternately with the water. Spread into the tin and bake for 50–60 minutes or until cooked when tested with a skewer. Cover with glacé icing and decorate with cherries.

CHERRY CAKE 3

Makes: 1 x 20 cm (8 in) round or square cake

105 g (3½ oz/½ cup) glacé cherries

Plain flour, to dust

175 g (6 oz) butter, softened

165 g (5¾ oz/¾ cup) sugar

3 eggs

225 g (8 oz/1½ cups) plain flour

1 teaspoon baking powder

1 teaspoon finely grated lemon zest

Approximately 2 tablespoons milk

1 Preheat oven to 170°C (325°F/Gas 3). Grease a 20 cm (8 in) round or square cake tin and line base with baking paper. Cut the cherries into three pieces and toss them in a little flour to coat lightly (this prevents them from sticking together and sinking to the bottom of the mixture).

2 Cream the butter and sugar, add eggs one at a time, beating well after each addition. Slowly beat in the sifted flour, adding the baking powder with the last spoonful. Beat mixture thoroughly, add cherries and lemon zest and a little milk (if necessary). This should be a fairly stiff mixture.

3 Bake for 55 minutes or until cooked when tested with a skewer.

THE LAND
COOKERY CONTEST
1967-68

Over $600 in Prizes

CONDUCTED FOR THE COUNTRY WOMEN'S ASSOCIATION OF N.S.W.

1967–68 Schedule cover. Image courtesy of the CWA.

FRUIT AND VEGETABLE CAKES

RICH FRUIT CAKE

First judged in 1967

Makes: 1 x 20 cm (8 in) round cake

Points to be looked for in judging: Smooth, even top, well risen and slightly rounded towards the centre, but not peaked. Smooth, even sides, with no white patches or blotches on the surface.

Browned evenly on sides, top and bottom. Texture should be firm and even, with no holes or tunnels; moist, but not heavy or doughy. Fruit should be evenly distributed, and a good balance of fruit and mixture apparent.

Should not be overflavoured with spices and essences so that the natural flavour of the fruits is lost.

From Schedule of 1966–67

255 g (9¼ oz/1½ cups) sultanas

255 g (9¼ oz/1¾ cups) currants

255 g (9¼ oz/1½ cups) chopped raisins

80 g (2¾ oz/⅓ cup) chopped red glacé cherries

120 g (4¼ oz/¾ cup) mixed peel

110 g (3¾ oz/⅔ cup) blanched almonds, chopped

80 ml (2½ fl oz/⅓ cup) sherry or brandy

250 g (9¼ oz/1⅔ cups) plain flour

50 g (1¾ oz/⅓ cup) self-raising flour

¼ teaspoon ground nutmeg

½ teaspoon ground cloves

½ teaspoon ground ginger

250 g (9 oz) butter, softened

245 g (9 oz/1⅓ cups, lightly packed) brown sugar

½ teaspoon lemon essence or finely grated lemon zest

½ teaspoon vanilla essence

½ teaspoon almond essence

4 large eggs

Central Western Group Conference, June 1973. Photo courtesy of the CWA.

1 Mix together all the fruit and nuts and sprinkle with sherry or brandy. Cover and leave for at least 1 hour, preferably overnight.

2 Preheat oven to 160°C (315°F/Gas 2–3). Grease a deep 20 cm (8 in) round cake tin and line base and side with two layers of brown paper and then a layer of baking paper. Sift together the flours and spices.

3 Cream butter, sugar and essences. Add eggs one at a time, beating well after each, then alternately add fruit and flour mixtures. Mix thoroughly—the mixture should be stiff enough to support a wooden spoon.

4 Place mixture into the prepared tin, smooth the surface and bake for about 3½–4 hours. Allow the cake to cool in tin.

Tip: To ensure uniformity it is suggested the raisins be chopped into 2–3 pieces, cherries into 4–6 pieces and almonds into 3–4 pieces.

FRUIT CAKE

First judged in 1952

Makes: 1 x 20 cm (8 in) round or square cake

255 g (9¼ oz/1½ cups) sultanas

255 g (9¼ oz/1¾ cups) currants

120 g (4¼ oz/⅔ cup) chopped raisins

60 g (2¼ oz/¼ cup) red glacé cherries

40 g (1½ oz/¼ cup) mixed peel

100 g (3½ oz/⅔ cup) blanched almonds, chopped

30 g (1 oz) orange marmalade

1 dessertspoon finely grated orange zest

1 teaspoon finely grated lemon zest

30 ml (1 fl oz) lemon juice

80 ml (2½ fl oz/⅓ cup) brandy

250 g (9 oz) butter, softened

245 g (9 oz/1⅓ cups, lightly packed) brown sugar

4 eggs

185 g (6½ oz/1¼ cups) plain flour

50 g (1¾ oz/⅓ cup) self-raising flour

1. Combine fruit, almonds, marmalade, orange and lemon zests, juice and brandy in a large bowl. Mix well. Cover bowl and stand for up to 1 week.

2. Preheat oven to 150°C (300°F/Gas 2). Grease a deep 20 cm (8 in) round or square cake tin and line base and side(s) with two layers of brown paper and then a layer of baking paper.

3. Cream the butter and sugar only until combined. Beat eggs in, one at a time. Beat only until combined after each addition of egg. Add the creamed mixture to fruit. Mix well then stir in sifted flours in two batches.

4. Spread mixture evenly into the prepared tin. Bake for about 3 hours or until cooked when tested with a skewer.

LIGHT FRUIT CAKE

First judged in 1952

Makes: 1 x 20 cm (8 in) round cake

Should be light in colour and evenly cooked on top, sides and bottom. Texture should be firm, with no holes or tunnels; moist, but not heavy or doughy. Fruit should be evenly distributed.

From Schedule of 1960–61

450 g (1 lb/3 cups) plain flour

1 teaspoon baking powder

250 g (9 oz) butter, softened

220 g (7¾ oz/1 cup) caster sugar

4 large eggs

1 teaspoon vanilla essence

Pinch of salt

370 g (13 oz/2 cups) mixed dried fruit

1 Preheat oven to 160°C (315°F/Gas 2–3). Grease and line a deep 20 cm (8 in) round cake tin. Sift flour and baking powder together.

2 Combine butter, sugar, eggs, vanilla and salt in a large bowl and beat until creamy. Add mixed fruit and flour mixture and stir to combine.

3 Place in the prepared tin and smooth the surface. Bake for 1¾ hours or until cooked when tested with a skewer. Cool in the tin.

BOILED FRUIT CAKE

First judged in 1992

Makes: 1 x 20 cm (8 in) round cake

To be cooked in 20 cm tin.
From Schedule of 1991–92

170 g (5¾ oz/1 cup) seeded raisins

160 g (5½ oz/1 cup) whole pitted dates

170 g (5¾ oz/1 cup) sultanas

60 g (2¼ oz/½ cup) chopped walnuts

1 tablespoon mixed peel

500 ml (17 fl oz/2 cups) water

115 g (4 oz) butter, cubed

3 eggs

220 g (7¾ oz/1 cup) sugar

300 g (10½ oz/2 cups) plain flour

1 teaspoon mixed spice

½ teaspoon ground nutmeg

1 teaspoon ground cinnamon

2 teaspoons cream of tartar

1 teaspoon bicarbonate of soda

Chocolate icing, to serve

Walnuts, to decorate

1 Preheat oven to moderate (180°C/350°F/Gas 4). Grease and line a deep 20 cm (8 in) round cake tin. Put the raisins, dates, sultanas, walnuts and peel in a saucepan with the water and boil slowly for 10 minutes. Add butter. Cool the fruit.

2 Beat eggs and sugar until well creamed. Add the well-sifted flour to the sugar and eggs, then add the mixed spice, nutmeg and cinnamon, cream of tartar and bicarbonate of soda; then add boiled fruit and stir well to combine.

3 Spoon into the prepared tin and smooth surface. Bake for 1 hour–1¼ hours or until cooked when tested with a skewer. When cold, ice with chocolate icing and decorate with walnuts.

GLUTEN-FREE FRUIT CAKE

First judged in 2009

Makes: 1 x 20 cm (8 in) round or square cake

To be cooked in 20 cm tin. No icing.
From Schedule of 2008–09

510 g (1 lb 2 oz/2¾ cups) mixed
  dried fruit
125 g (4½ oz) butter, cubed
220 g (7¾ oz/1 cup) sugar
1 teaspoon mixed spice
185 ml (6 fl oz/¾ cup) water
1 teaspoon bicarbonate of soda

1 teaspoon gluten-free baking powder
2 eggs, whisked
125 g (4½ oz/1 cup) cornflour
160 g (5½ oz/1½ cups) soy flour
60 ml (2 fl oz/¼ cup) brandy or
  dark rum (optional)

1 Preheat oven to moderate (180°C/350°F/Gas 4). Grease a 20 cm (8 in) round or square cake tin and line base with baking paper. Combine in a saucepan the mixed fruit, butter, sugar, mixed spice and add the water. Bring to the boil and cook for 10 minutes.

2 Cool, then stir in bicarbonate of soda and baking powder. Stir in eggs, then combined and sifted cornflour and soy flour. Stir in the brandy or rum, if using.

3 Put in the prepared tin. Bake for 60–70 minutes or until cooked when tested with a skewer.

BOILED FRUIT PUDDING 1

First judged in 1963

Makes: 1 boiled fruit pudding

Points to be looked for: Fruit evenly cut, flavour rich and mellow. Should have sultanas, currants, raisins, peel. Dates allowed, but NOT cherries. Should be dark but not overdone.

A good shape with no holes, no soggy, wet or mouldy patches.

From Schedule of 1988–89

255 g (9¼ oz/1½ cups) sultanas,
  chopped
260 g (9¼ oz/1⅔ cups) mixed peel
255 g (9¼ oz/1½ cups) raisins, chopped
115 g (4 oz/¾ cup) currants
100 ml (3½ fl oz) dark rum
250 g (9 oz) butter, softened
245 g (9 oz/1⅓ cups, lightly packed)
  brown sugar

5 eggs
150 g (5½ oz/1 cup) plain flour
1 teaspoon mixed spice
½ teaspoon ground nutmeg
½ teaspoon bicarbonate of soda
Pinch of salt
120 g (4¼ oz/2 cups, lightly packed)
  fresh soft white breadcrumbs

1   Prepare pudding cloth (see opposite). Combine all the fruit in a bowl and stir through the rum.

2   In a large bowl, cream the butter and sugar. Add eggs one at a time, beating well after each addition. Stir in prepared fruit and rum. Add sifted dry ingredients together with the breadcrumbs. Mix well.

3   Put into the prepared pudding cloth, fasten securely. Place into a saucepan of rapidly boiling water and boil steadily for 4½ hours. Top up with boiling water as necessary.

The Land Cookery Organisers: Miss G. Winch (left) and Mrs L. Hannigan of Broken Hill prepare for the display of delicious cakes, biscuits, etc from the State's top cooks, June 1973. Photo courtesy of the CWA.

Hints for boiled pudding:

* Boil calico cloth for 30 minutes, wring out and rub with flour. A cloth which has been used a number of times is more pliable and therefore less inclined to double over and show fold marks on the pudding.

* Pudding should be a good shape with dryness of surface. Colour good but not overdone, flavour rich and mellow.

* Cut raisins, sultanas and peel to the same size as currants.

BOILED FRUIT PUDDING 2

First judged in 1963

Makes: 1 boiled fruit pudding

Important: In judging, the method of cutting right through the centre of the pudding must be observed. Competitors must observe the ¹/₂ lb shortening basis as standard mixture for size and weight.

Points to be looked for in judging: A good rounded shape, with no holes or ridges in the mixture from fold of pudding cloth. There should be no soggy, wet or mouldy patches. The pudding should have a rich dark colour, and colour should be even all through. Should have a good, well-balanced fruity flavour with no predominating flavour from bicarbonate of soda.

From Schedule of 1970–71

255 g (9¹/₄ oz/1¹/₂ cups) sultanas

255 g (9¹/₄ oz/1¹/₂ cups) raisins

255 g (9¹/₄ oz/1³/₄ cups) currants

125 g (4¹/₂ oz/²/₃ cup) chopped dried figs

120 g (4¹/₄ oz/³/₄ cup) chopped dates

120 g (4¹/₄ oz/³/₄ cup) mixed peel

250 g (9 oz) butter, softened

245 g (9 oz/1¹/₃ cup, lightly packed) brown sugar

1 teaspoon finely grated orange zest

1 teaspoon finely grated lemon zest

5 eggs

120 g (4¹/₄ oz/2 cups, lightly packed) fresh breadcrumbs

50 g (1³/₄ oz) chopped preserved ginger

1 grated apple

225 g (8 oz/1¹/₂ cups) plain flour

1 teaspoon bicarbonate of soda

1 teaspoon salt

1 teaspoon ground cloves

1 teaspoon ground nutmeg

1 teaspoon ground cinnamon

1   Prepare pudding cloth. (See Boiled Fruit Pudding 1, Hints, page 85.) Mix all the dried fruit and peel together. Cream butter, sugar and orange and lemon zests until pale and creamy. Add eggs one at a time, mixing well after each addition. Add breadcrumbs, ginger and apple.

2   Sift dry ingredients together and fold in alternately with the fruit. Mix well, put onto pudding cloth, fasten securely. Place into a large saucepan of rapidly boiling water, boil steadily for 5–6 hours. Top up with boiling water as necessary.

STEAMED FRUIT PUDDING

First judged in 1967

Makes: 1 steamed fruit pudding

Important: In judging, the method of cutting right through the centre of the pudding must be observed. Competitors must observe the ¹/₂ lb shortening basis as standard mixture for size and weight.

Points to be looked for in judging: The pudding should have a rich dark colour, and colour should be even throughout. There should be no holes in the mixture and no soggy, wet or mouldy patches. It should have a good well-balanced fruity flavour.

From Schedule of 1969–70

245 g (9 oz/1½ cups) pitted dates,
    chopped

255 g (9¼ oz/1½ cups) raisins

255 g (9¼ oz/1½ cups) sultanas

115 g (4 oz/¾ cup) currants

120 g (4¼ oz/¾ cup) mixed peel

1 small carrot, grated

2 tablespoons brandy or spirits

250 g (9 oz) butter, softened

220 g (7¾ oz/1 cup, firmly packed)
    brown sugar

1 tablespoon finely grated orange zest

1 tablespoon finely grated lemon zest

4 eggs

1 small apple, grated

120 g (4¼ oz/2 cups, lightly packed)
    fresh breadcrumbs (4 days old)

225 g (8 oz/1½ cups) plain flour

1 teaspoon mixed spice

½ teaspoon ground nutmeg

½ teaspoon bicarbonate of soda

Pinch of salt

1 Grease a 2.5 litre (87 fl oz/10-cup) pudding basin (mould) or steamer. Soak dried fruit and carrot in brandy overnight in a large bowl. Cream butter, sugar and orange and lemon zests in a large bowl until pale and creamy. Add eggs one at a time, beating well after each addition.

2 Stir in the soaked fruit, grated apple and breadcrumbs. Sift the dry ingredients together, fold carefully into fruit mixture and mix until well combined.

3 Spoon into the prepared pudding basin or steamer, filling basin to two-thirds full. Put a piece of foil over, clip on lid. Put into a large saucepan and pour in boiling water. Cover saucepan and steam for 3 hours. Top up with water as necessary.

State Champions (left to right): Mrs A. Scholz (Terramungamine), Orange Cake;
Mrs P. Hammon (Hazelbrook-Woodford), home-made sweets; and Mrs A. Wooding (Taree),
who won both plain and fancy assorted biscuits, June 1959. Photo courtesy of *The Land*.

BUSHMAN'S BROWNIE

First judged in 1952

Makes: 16 squares

600 g (1 lb 5 oz/4 cups) plain flour
1 teaspoon bicarbonate of soda
1 teaspoon cream of tartar
1 teaspoon mixed spice
1 teaspoon ground cinnamon

250 g (9 oz) butter, chopped
220 g (7¾ oz/1 cup) sugar
140 g (5 oz/1 cup) currants
170 g (5¾ oz/1 cup) raisins
Sufficient milk to mix

1   Preheat oven to moderate (180°C/350°F/Gas 4). Grease a 23 cm (9 in) square cake tin.

2   Sift the flour in a bowl with the bicarbonate of soda, cream of tartar, mixed spice and cinnamon. Rub in the butter with your fingertips until crumbly.

3   Add the sugar, currants and raisins and mix with the milk to make a dough slightly stiffer than that of fruit cake. Spread evenly into the prepared tin and bake for 1 hour.

Note: This recipe was originally made with dripping instead of butter.

BROWNIE

First judged in 1952

Makes: 16 squares

Has taken many prizes at Dubbo Show.

250 g (9 oz) butter, softened

185 g (6½ oz/1 cup, lightly packed) brown sugar

2 eggs

150 g (5½ oz/1 cup) plain flour

300 g (10½ oz/2 cups) self-raising flour

1 teaspoon ground nutmeg

1 teaspoon ground cinnamon

Pinch of salt

250 ml (9 fl oz/1 cup) milk

140 g (5 oz/1 cup) currants

170 g (5¾ oz/1 cup) sultanas

1 Preheat oven to 200°C (400°F/Gas 6). Grease a 23 cm (9 in) square cake tin and line base with baking paper.

2 Beat the butter and sugar together until creamy. Add eggs one at a time and beat well. Sift together the flours with the spices and salt.

3 Gradually mix the sifted flour and milk into the creamed mixture. Lastly stir in the fruit.

4 Spread evenly into the prepared tin. Bake for 1 hour–1¼ hours or until cooked when tested with a skewer. Cut into squares when cold.

Tip: A little cut-up mixed peel may be added if liked. This recipe was originally made with dripping instead of butter.

BOWRA BROWNIE

First judged in 1952

Makes: 20 cm (8 in) square cake

450 g (1 lb/3 cups) plain flour
2 teaspoons baking powder
2 teaspoons ground cinnamon
Pinch of salt
110 g (3¾ oz/½ cup) sugar

1 large tablespoon butter
1 egg, whisked
250 ml (9 fl oz/1 cup) milk
1 tablespoon treacle
120 g (4¼ oz/⅔ cup) sultanas

1   Preheat oven to moderate (180°C/350°F/Gas 4). Grease and line a 20 cm (8 in) square cake tin.

2   Sift the dry ingredients together then stir in the sugar. Rub in the butter. Combine the wet ingredients and stir them in. Add the sultanas and stir to combine.

3   Spread evenly into the prepared tin. Bake for 50–60 minutes. Cool in the tin.

Tip: This is nicest when not too fresh, cut in slices and buttered.

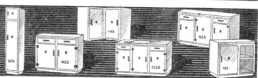

SULTANA CAKE

First judged in 1963

Makes: 1 x 20 cm (8 in) square or round cake

Appearance: should be light in colour and evenly cooked on top, sides and bottom. Texture should be firm, with no holes or tunnels; moist but not heavy our doughy. Fruit should be evenly distributed. The following recipe has been suggested as a guide by the CWA, but need not necessarily be followed.

From Schedule of 1962–63

---

225 g (8 oz) butter, softened
220 g (7¾ oz/1 cup) caster sugar
3 eggs
350 g (12 oz/2⅓ cups) plain flour
1½ teaspoons baking powder

Pinch of salt
340 g (11¾ oz/2 cups) sultanas
125 ml (4 fl oz/½ cup) milk, flavoured
   with vanilla or lemon essence (only a
   few drops if lemon is used)

1   Preheat oven to moderate (180°C/350°F/Gas 4). Grease a 20 cm (8 in) square or round cake tin and line with baking paper.

2   Cream the butter and sugar together. Add eggs, one at a time, beating well to combine. Sift the flour, baking powder and salt together three times. Dust sultanas with a little of the measured flour mixture.

3   Add the flour, sultanas and milk alternately to the creamed mixture. Mix all together lightly and well.

4   Pour the mixture into the prepared tin and smooth the surface. Bake for 1¼ hours or until cooked when tested with a skewer. Leave in the tin to cool.

BOILED RAISIN CHOCOLATE CAKE

First judged in 2009

Makes: 1 x 20 cm (8 in) square or round cake

To be cooked in 20 cm tin. Chocolate icing on top. No decoration.
From Schedule of 2009–10

255 g (9¼ oz/1½ cups) raisins

375 ml (13 fl oz/1½ cups) water

1 teaspoon bicarbonate of soda

30 g (1 oz/¼ cup) cocoa powder, sifted

1½ teaspoons ground cinnamon

¼ teaspoon ground cloves

1 teaspoon vanilla essence

200 g (7 oz) butter, softened

220 g (7¾ oz/1 cup) caster sugar

3 eggs

185 g (6½ oz/1¼ cups) plain flour

110 g (3¾ oz/¾ cup) self-raising flour

Chocolate icing, to serve

1 Preheat oven to moderate (180°C/350°F/Gas 4). Grease a 20 cm (8 in) square or round cake tin and line base with baking paper.

2 Combine raisins and the water in saucepan, bring to the boil. Reduce heat, simmer uncovered for 10 minutes. Remove from heat, stir in bicarbonate of soda, cocoa, spices and vanilla. Cool to room temperature.

3 Beat the butter and sugar till pale and creamy, add eggs one at a time, beating until just combined. Stir in combined sifted flours and raisin mixture in two batches. Spread mixture into the prepared tin.

4 Bake for about 1 hour 10 minutes or until cooked when tested with a skewer. Stand 5 minutes. Turn out to cool. Ice with chocolate icing.

KENTISH CAKE

First judged in 2001

Makes: 1 x 20 cm (8 in) round cake

To be cooked in 20 cm round tin, iced on top only with chocolate icing.
From Schedule of 2000–01

170 g (5¾ oz) butter, softened

165 g (5¾ oz/¾ cup) sugar

2 eggs

150 g (5½ oz/1 cup) self-raising flour

2 tablespoons cocoa powder

2 tablespoons desiccated coconut

60 ml (2 fl oz/¼ cup) milk

95 g (3¼ oz/½ cup) mixed dried fruit and/or glacé fruit and nuts (such as cherries and walnuts)

Chocolate icing, to serve

1 Preheat oven to moderate (180°C/350°F/Gas 4). Grease a 20 cm (8 in) round cake tin and line base with baking paper.

2 Cream the butter and sugar, then add eggs, beating well after each addition. Fold in sifted flour and cocoa and the coconut. Stir in the milk and mixed fruit and nuts.

3 Spoon into the prepared tin and bake for 45 minutes or until cooked when tested with a skewer. When cool, ice with chocolate icing.

Early days at the Mudgee Rest Room. Photo courtesy of CWA.

PRUNE CAKE 1

First judged in 2003

Makes: 1 x 18 cm (7 in) round cake

250 ml (9 fl oz/1 cup) boiling water

250 g (9 oz/1 cup) chopped prunes, cut
  into small pieces

300 g (10½ oz/2 cups) self-raising flour

1½ teaspoons bicarbonate of soda

1 teaspoon ground cinnamon

1 teaspoon ground ginger

1 teaspoon ground nutmeg

1 teaspoon salt

330 g (11¾ oz/1½ cups) sugar

125 ml (4 fl oz/½ cup) vegetable oil
  (such as safflower or sunflower)

3 eggs

125 g (4½ oz/1 cup) chopped nuts
  (such as walnuts or pecans)

1 Preheat oven to moderate (180°C/350°F/Gas 4). Grease an 18 cm (7 in)
   round cake tin and line base with baking paper. Pour the boiling water over
   prunes and let stand 2 hours.

2 Sift the flour, bicarbonate of soda, spices and salt into a bowl, stir through
   the sugar. Add prunes, oil and eggs. Blend thoroughly. Beat for 2 minutes at
   medium speed. Stir through the nuts.

3 Pour into the prepared tin, bake for about 45–55 minutes. Cool
   on a wire rack.

PRUNE CAKE 2

First judged in 2003

Makes: 1 x 18 cm (7 in) round cake

14 pitted prunes
125 g (4½ oz) butter, softened
165 g (5¾ oz/¾ cup) sugar
2 eggs
185 g (6½ oz/1¼ cups) self-raising flour
1 teaspoon cocoa powder
¼ teaspoon ground cloves
¼ teaspoon ground nutmeg
¼ teaspoon ground cinnamon

Lemon icing
2 tablespoons milk, at room temperature
2 teaspoons lemon juice
2 teaspoons butter, softened
210 g (7½ oz/1⅔ cups) icing sugar
1 teaspoon finely grated lemon zest

1   Preheat oven to moderate (180°C/350°F/Gas 4). Grease an 18 cm (7 in) round cake tin and line base with baking paper. Put the prunes in a saucepan with enough water to cover, simmer for 10 minutes or until soft then drain and halve prunes (keep 4 tablespoons of the prune cooking juice).

2   Cream butter and sugar, add eggs and beat well to combine. Sift together the flour, cocoa and spices and fold into the butter mixture. Fold in prunes and reserved prune juice.

3   Spoon into the prepared tin. Bake for about 45 minutes.

4   To make the lemon icing, combine milk, lemon juice, butter and sifted icing sugar and beat well. Add lemon zest last. Add more icing sugar or more milk, to thicken or thin respectively. Ice cooled cake on top with icing.

Mrs C. Kerr and Mrs C. Devenish at Woodstock branch, judging entries, 1956. Mrs Devenish has been a consistent winner in the competition for five years. Photo courtesy of *The Land*.

DIABETIC MANGO FRUIT CAKE

First judged in 2007

Makes: 1 x 20 cm (8 in) round or square cake

To be cooked in 20 cm tin. No icing.
From Schedule of 2007–08

425 g (15 oz) tin mangoes with liquid

*430 g (15¼ oz/2⅓ cups) mixed
    dried fruit*

1½ teaspoons bicarbonate of soda

2 eggs

1 teaspoon vanilla essence

225 g (8 oz/1½ cups) self-raising flour

½ teaspoon mixed spice

1   Preheat oven to 170°C (325°F/Gas 3). Grease a 20 cm (8 in) round or square cake tin and line base with baking paper.

2   In a large saucepan boil together the mango with liquid and the mixed fruit for 3–4 minutes. Mash the mango. Add bicarbonate of soda and leave to cool.

3   Beat the eggs and vanilla well and add to the mango and fruit mixture, then stir through the flour and mixed spice.

4   Place in the prepared tin and bake for 1 hour or a little less. Bake until cooked when tested with a skewer.

CARROT CAKE

First judged in 1985

Makes: 1 loaf

To be cooked in a loaf tin. Iced on top only with white butter icing. No decorations allowed. Chopped nuts allowed.

Hints to the competitor: Texture and cooking to be even and of good keeping quality.

From Schedule of 1984–85

3 eggs

220 g (7¾ oz/1 cup) sugar

185 ml (6 fl oz/¾ cup) vegetable oil (such as safflower or sunflower)

225 g (8 oz/1½ cups) plain flour

2 teaspoons ground cinnamon

1½ teaspoons baking powder

1 teaspoon bicarbonate of soda

310 g (11 oz/2 cups, firmly packed) grated carrot

1½ teaspoons vanilla essence

White butter icing, to serve

1   Preheat oven to 150°C (300°F/Gas 2). Grease an 11 x 21 cm (4¼ x 8¼ in) loaf tin and line base with baking paper.

2   Beat eggs and sugar. Slowly add oil, then the combined and sifted flour, cinnamon, baking powder and bicarbonate of soda. Beat well, add carrot and vanilla and combine well.

3   Place in the prepared tin and bake for 1 hour or until cooked when tested with a skewer. When cool, ice with white butter icing.

1957–58 Schedule cover. Image courtesy of the CWA.

BEETROOT CAKE

First judged in 2005

Makes: 1 x 20 cm (8 in) round cake

To be cooked in 20 cm round tin. Iced on top only with chocolate icing. No fruit allowed.
From Schedule of 2004–05

225 g (8 oz/1½ cups) plain flour
55 g (2 oz/½ cup) cocoa powder
1½ teaspoons baking powder
330 g (11¾ oz/1½ cups) caster sugar
250 ml (9 fl oz/1 cup) vegetable oil
   (such as sunflower or canola)

1 teaspoon vanilla essence
3 large eggs
200 g (7 oz/1 cup) cooked, peeled and
   mashed or puréed beetroot
Chocolate icing, to serve

1   Preheat oven to 150°C (300°F/Gas 2). Grease a 20 cm (8 in) round cake tin and line base with baking paper.

2   Sift the flour, cocoa and baking powder into a bowl. Stir in the sugar.

3   In another bowl, mix together the oil, vanilla, eggs and beetroot. Mix in the dry ingredients. Pour the mixture into the prepared tin and bake until the cake is firm to touch and well risen, about 60 minutes. Cool. Ice with chocolate icing.

PUMPKIN DATE CAKE

First judged in 2007

Makes: 1 x 20 cm (8 in) round cake

To be cooked in 20 cm tin. No icing on top.
From Schedule of 2007–08

250 g (9 oz) butter, softened
160 g (5½ oz/¾ cup) caster sugar
1 tablespoon finely grated orange zest
2 eggs
160 g (5½ oz/1 cup) chopped dates

45 g (1¾ oz/½ cup) desiccated coconut
125 g (4½ oz/½ cup) cold cooked and
  mashed pumpkin
300 g (10½ oz/2 cups) self-raising flour
125 ml (4 fl oz/½ cup) milk

1   Preheat oven to 170°C (325°F/Gas 3). Grease a deep 20 cm (8 in) round
    cake tin and line base with baking paper.

2   Cream butter, sugar and orange zest in a small bowl until pale and creamy,
    beat in eggs one at a time, until combined.

3   Transfer mixture to a larger bowl, stir in the dates, coconut and pumpkin.
    Stir in half the sifted flour and half the milk, and then stir in remainder
    of the flour and the milk.

4   Spread into the prepared tin. Bake for about 1½ hours or until cooked
    when tested. Allow to stand 5 minutes before turning out.

PUMPKIN FRUIT CAKE 1

First judged in 1987

Makes: 1 x 20 cm (8 in) square or round cake

Cakes should be good colour and keeping quality, nuts allowed. 20 cm tin to be used.
From Schedule of 1987–88

250 g (9 oz) butter, softened
220 g (7¾ oz/1 cup) sugar
2 eggs
250 g (9 oz/1 cup) cold cooked and
   mashed pumpkin

510 g (1 lb 2 oz/2¾ cups) mixed dried
   fruit
300 g (10½ oz/2 cups) self-raising flour
1 teaspoon ground cinnamon

1   Preheat oven to moderate (180°C/350°F/Gas 4). Grease a 20 cm (8 in) square or round cake tin and line base with baking paper.

2   Beat butter and sugar to a cream. Add eggs one at a time, beating well after each addition. Add pumpkin, fruit and sifted flour and cinnamon alternately. Mix until well combined.

3   Spoon into the prepared tin and smooth surface. Bake for about 1½ hours or until cooked when tested. Cool in tin.

PUMPKIN FRUIT CAKE 2

First judged in 1987

Makes: 1 x 20 cm (8 in) square or round cake

3 tablespoons margarine

165 g (5¾ oz/¾ cup) sugar

1 teaspoon vanilla essence

250 g (9 oz/1 cup) cold cooked and
  mashed pumpkin

125 ml (4 fl oz/½ cup) milk

300 g (10½ oz/2 cups) self-raising flour

Pinch of salt

185 g (6½ oz/1 cup) mixed dried fruit

1 Preheat oven to moderate (180°C/350°F/Gas 4). Grease a 20 cm (8 in) square or round cake tin and line base with baking paper.

2 Cream margarine and sugar in a bowl, add vanilla and mashed pumpkin. Mix well, then add milk and sifted flour and salt, alternately. Lastly stir in the fruit and stir until well mixed.

3 Spoon into the prepared tin and smooth the surface. Bake for 60–70 minutes (test it after 1 hour). When cool, ice, if liked.

THE LAND
COOKERY CONTEST
1966-67

Over $600 in Prizes

CONDUCTED FOR THE COUNTRY WOMEN'S ASSOCIATION OF N.S.W.

1966–67 Schedule cover. Image courtesy of the CWA.

BISCUITS, SLICES, MERINGUES AND PIKELETS

ANZAC BISCUITS

First judged in 1981

Makes: about 40 biscuits

To be cooked. Approximately 7 cm in size. Six biscuits to be displayed on plate provided.
From Schedule of 2004–05

95 g (3¼ oz/1 cup) rolled oats

90 g (3¼ oz/1 cup) desiccated coconut

150 g (5½ oz/1 cup) plain flour

220 g (7¾ oz/1 cup) sugar

½ teaspoon salt

125 g (4½ oz) butter

1 tablespoon golden syrup

1 teaspoon bicarbonate of soda

2 tablespoons boiling water

1   Preheat oven to moderate (180°C/350°F/Gas 4). Grease two baking trays.

2   Place the oats, coconut, sifted flour, sugar and salt into a bowl. Mix well. Melt butter, add golden syrup, bicarbonate of soda and the boiling water. Stir well. Add liquid ingredients to dry ingredients. Mix well.

3   Place mixture in spoonfuls onto the prepared trays and bake for 10–12 minutes. Remove from oven, loosen biscuits on tray with a knife or spatula. Allow to cool on tray.

1914 ANZAC BISCUITS

First judged in 1981

Makes: 40–50 biscuits

190 g (6¾ oz/2 cups) rolled oats
150 g (5½ oz/1 cup) plain flour
165 g (5¾ oz/¾ cup) sugar
125 g (4½ oz) butter, cubed

1 large rounded tablespoon golden syrup
1 teaspoon bicarbonate of soda
2 tablespoons hot water

1 Preheat oven to 160°C (315°F/Gas 2–3). Grease two baking trays.

2 Mix together the oats, flour and sugar in a bowl. Melt the butter and golden syrup together, add bicarbonate of soda dissolved in the hot water. Pour into the dry ingredients and mix well.

3 Roll into balls the size of a walnut (or a 10-cent piece) and place on the prepared trays. Bake for about 20 minutes until golden. Move biscuit positions while hot. Allow to cool and crisp on tray.

PLAIN BISCUITS

First judged in 1952

Makes: 40–50 biscuits

Can have ingredients added to mixture but nothing to outside.

May be any fancy shape, but not joined together with icing in a sandwich style. Crystallised fruits, nuts, etc., baked in with the mixture may be included in this class.

From Schedule of 1962–63

Crisp Biscuits

Makes: 40–50 biscuits that are twice the size of a penny

550 g (1 lb 4 oz/3⅔ cups) plain flour

Pinch of salt

175 g (6 oz) butter

50 g (1¾ oz/½ cup) ground almonds

A little milk or water

1 Preheat oven to moderate (180°C/350°F/Gas 4). Leave ungreased a large baking tray.

2 Sift the flour and salt into a bowl and rub in the butter until the mixture resembles fine breadcrumbs. Add ground almonds, then stir through a little milk or water to make a firm dough. Set aside for 30 minutes.

3 Take small balls of dough and press into flattened rounds using the palm of your hand. Place on the tray. Bake for 15–20 minutes. Cool on a wire rack.

Lemon and Almond Biscuits

Makes: about 25 biscuits

125 g (4½ oz) butter, softened
75 g (2¾ oz/⅓ cup) sugar
1 teaspoon finely grated lemon zest
½ teaspoon vanilla essence
150 g (5½ oz/1 cup) plain flour
50 g (1¾ oz/½ cup) ground almonds
120 g (4¼ oz/¾ cup) blanched almonds, toasted and chopped
Extra sugar

1   Preheat oven to 170°C (325°F/Gas 3). Lightly grease a large baking tray.

2   Beat the butter, add the sugar and beat until pale and creamy. Add lemon zest and vanilla. Stir in sifted flour, ground almonds and toasted almonds.

3   Turn out onto a lightly floured surface and roll the mixture into a log about 5 cm (2 in) in diameter. Chill for 30 minutes then roll in extra sugar. Cut into about 1 cm (½ in) slices. Bake for about 15 minutes. Move position on tray and allow to cool on tray.

Basic Biscuits

Makes: 30–40 biscuits

225 g (8 oz/1½ cups) self-raising flour
70 g (2½ oz/½ cup) custard powder
Pinch of salt
110 g (3¾ oz/½ cup) sugar
125 g (4½ oz) butter
60 ml (2 fl oz/¼ cup) milk

1   Preheat oven to 160°C (315°F/Gas 2–3). Lightly grease two baking trays.

2   Sift the flour, custard powder and salt into a bowl, add sugar. Rub in the butter until mixture is like breadcrumbs. Add milk and mix firmly by hand (a little extra milk is sometimes needed in cold weather).

3   Turn out onto a floured board, knead lightly to coat with a little flour. Roll out thinly to 5 mm (¼ in) thick, cut to desired shapes. Place on the prepared trays. Bake for 12–15 minutes or until a pale straw colour. Move positions on tray and allow to cool on tray to crisp up.

Variations

Chocolate cookies —add 2 tablespoons cocoa powder or 60 g (2¼ oz/⅓ cup) chocolate chips and a little extra milk. Drop dough in rough heaps without rolling (about 1–2 teaspoons).

Cherry and nut drops —add 60 g (2¼ oz/¼ cup) chopped glacé cherries and 60 g (2¼ oz/½ cup) chopped walnuts or peanuts. Drop dough in rough heaps without rolling.

Coconut roughs —add 45 g (1¾ oz/½ cup) desiccated coconut and a little extra milk. Drop dough in rough heaps without rolling.

Spicy date drops —add ½ teaspoon ground cinnamon, ¼ teaspoon ground nutmeg with the flour and 80 g (2¾ oz/½ cup) chopped dates with a little extra milk. Drop dough in rough heaps.

Crunchy Peanut Cookies

Makes: 30–40 biscuits

110 g (3¾ oz/¾ cup) self-raising flour

½ teaspoon mixed spice

¼ teaspoon bicarbonate of soda

165 g (5¾ oz/¾ cup) caster sugar

50 g (1¾ oz/½ cup) rolled oats

30 g (1 oz/⅓ cup) desiccated coconut

1 teaspoon finely grated orange zest

140 g (5 oz/½ cup) crunchy peanut butter

1 tablespoon golden syrup

2–3 tablespoons milk

1 Preheat oven to 170°C (325°F/Gas 3). Lightly grease two baking trays. Sift the flour, mixed spice and bicarbonate of soda into a bowl. Stir in the sugar, oats, coconut and orange zest. Rub peanut butter into the dry ingredients until mixture is crumbly.

2 Mix the golden syrup with 2 tablespoons milk, add to mixture, stirring to make a soft dough (add a little more milk if needed). Turn out onto a lightly floured board and form into a smooth ball. Wrap in plastic wrap and refrigerate for 20 minutes.

3 Roll out dough to 5 mm (¼ in) thickness, cut to desired shapes. Place on the prepared trays. Bake for 8–10 minutes. Move position on trays and allow to cool and crisp on trays.

FANCY BISCUITS

First judged in 1952

Either iced or has cream between two layers.

Sandwich types, with cream filling, or iced and decorated biscuits. Decorative mixtures may be shaped or put through a forcing pipe.

Appearance: Shape and daintiness, variety of mixtures and delicacy of colour are the main factors for judging.

Baking: Bake to a golden brown in colour, depending on variety.

Flavour: Suitable to type of biscuit.

Important: Biscuits must be displayed in boxes measuring 10 x 14 inches and containers will be sold with biscuits. Contestants using larger boxes will be disqualified. Not less than six different mixtures can be entered in each class.

From Schedule of 1962–63

Yo Yo Biscuits

Makes: about 20 biscuits

90 g (3¼ oz) butter, softened
2 tablespoons icing sugar
110 g (3¾ oz/¾ cup) plain flour
2½ tablespoons custard powder
Raspberry jam

Butter filling

1 tablespoon soft butter
Approximately 6 tablespoons icing sugar
1 tablespoon custard powder

1 Preheat oven to moderate (180°C/350°F/Gas 4). Lightly grease two baking trays.

2 Cream the butter and sifted icing sugar in a bowl until pale and creamy. Sift together the flour and custard powder. Stir into the butter mixture and mix well.

3 Roll teaspoonfuls of mixture into small balls, put on the prepared trays, press each down lightly with the back of a fork. Bake for 10–15 minutes. Move position on tray and allow to cool on tray.

4 Make the butter filling by combining all ingredients to a smooth paste. Spread half the biscuits with a little jam and spread over the butter filling. Join biscuits together.

Brown Butter Biscuits

Makes: about 75 biscuits

250 g (9 oz) butter
220 g (7¾ oz/1 cup) sugar
2 teaspoons vanilla essence
2 eggs

410 g (14½ oz/2¾ cups) self-raising flour
Blanched whole almonds
Glacé cherries, halved

1 Preheat oven to 190°C (375°F/Gas 5). Lightly grease a large baking tray.

2 Put the butter in a saucepan and heat until golden brown. Remove from the heat and cool until butter starts to set.

3 Put the butter and sugar into a large bowl, beat until pale and creamy, add the vanilla then the eggs one at a time, mixing well. Mix in the sifted flour.

4 Roll into small balls, place on the prepared tray, flatten with a fork and place an almond or half a cherry on each. Bake for 12 minutes. Cool on trays.

Coffee Creams

Makes: 40–50 biscuits

125 g (4½ oz) butter, softened
110 g (3¾ oz/½ cup) sugar
1 egg, well whisked
1 tablespoon coffee essence
1 teaspoon vanilla essence
300 g (10½ oz/2 cups) plain flour
1 teaspoon bicarbonate of soda

Coffee icing
125 g (4½ oz/1 cup) icing sugar
1½ tablespoons butter, softened
Coffee essence, to flavour

1 Preheat oven to moderate (180°C/350°F/Gas 4). Lightly grease a large baking tray.

2 Cream butter and sugar in a bowl until pale and creamy. Add the egg, coffee and vanilla essences, beating well to combine. Sift together the flour and bicarbonate of soda. Add to the butter mixture and stir to a stiff dough.

3 Roll out very thinly and cut into shapes. Arrange on the prepared tray and bake for 10–15 minutes.

4 To make the icing, cream the icing sugar and butter in a bowl. Add enough coffee essence to flavour the icing and add a little hot water, if needed. Ice the cooled biscuits with the coffee icing.

Indian Coffee Creams

Makes: 25–30 joined biscuits

125 g (4½ oz) butter, softened
110 g (3¾ oz/½ cup) sugar
1 egg, whisked
1 tablespoon coffee essence
½ teaspoon vanilla essence
300 g (10½ oz/2 cups) self-raising flour
Egg wash (1 egg yolk combined with 2 teaspoons water)
Approximately 140 g (5 oz/1 cup) nuts, roughly chopped

Coffee filling
1 tablespoon butter, softened
125 g (4½ oz/1 cup) sifted icing sugar
Coffee essence, to taste

1   Preheat oven to moderate (180°C/350°F/Gas 4). Lightly grease a large baking tray.

2   Cream the butter and sugar in a bowl until pale and creamy. Add the egg, and coffee and vanilla essences, beating well. Sift in the flour and mix to a stiff dough.

3   Roll out the dough and cut into rounds. Brush half the rounds with egg wash and cover with nuts and leave remainder plain. Bake for 15–20 minutes.

4   To make the coffee filling, beat together the ingredients until smooth. When biscuits are cooled, join a plain base with a nutty-topped biscuit together with the filling.

Monte Carlos

Makes: about 36 joined biscuits

125 g (4½ oz) butter, softened
110 g (3¾ oz/½ cup) sugar
1 teaspoon vanilla essence
1 egg
1 tablespoon honey
350 g (12 oz/2⅓ cups) self-raising flour

Raspberry cream filling
2 level tablespoons butter, softened
125 g (4½ oz/1 cup) icing sugar, sifted
2 teaspoons raspberry jam
Vanilla essence, to flavour

1   Preheat oven to moderate (180°C/350°F/Gas 4). Lightly grease a large baking tray.

2   Cream the butter, sugar and vanilla until pale and creamy. Add the egg, beat well, then add the honey. Sift the flour and stir into the creamed mixture. Mix until smooth.

3   Place in teaspoonfuls on the prepared tray. Bake for about 10 minutes or until golden brown. Cool on tray.

4   To make the raspberry cream filling, cream together butter and icing sugar. Add jam and sufficient vanilla to flavour. Join cooled biscuits together with filling.

Lovely Twin Lakes (Zinc Corporation) was the setting for this friendly barbecue
get-together within the framework of a happy conference. CWA members (from left):
Mrs Roslyn Rodgers, Miss Ethel Constable (Bedgerabong), Mrs Pearl Lees (Bogan Gate),
Mrs Margaret Kennied (Bedgerabong) and Mrs Lila Hand (Yarrabandai), May 1973.
Photo courtesy of the CWA.

"*It keeps one pepped up — Goldenia Tea*"

SCOTCH SHORTBREAD

First judged in 1977

Makes: two 18 cm (7 in) sandwich tins

250 g (9 oz) butter, softened
75 g (2¾ oz/⅓ cup) caster sugar
335 g (11¾ oz/2¼ cups) plain flour
45 g (1¾ oz/¼ cup) ground rice or rice flour

1   Preheat oven to 160°C (315°F/Gas 2–3). Grease two 18 cm (7 in) sandwich tins.

2   Cream butter and sugar until light and creamy. Stir in sifted flours in two batches. When mixture becomes stiff, use hands to combine ingredients. Turn onto a lightly floured surface, then knead lightly until smooth.

3   Divide mixture between the prepared tins and evenly spread. Prick all over with a fork. Bake for 45 minutes. Stand for 10 minutes before removing from tins and placing on wire rack to cool.

MELT 'N' MIX SHORTBREAD

First judged in 2010

Makes: 24 shortbread fingers

Must be cooked. Six pieces approximately 6 x 3 cm in size.

From Schedule of 2009-10

250 g (9 oz) butter

55 g (2 oz/¼ cup) caster sugar

40 g (1½ oz/⅓ cup) icing sugar

40 g (1½ oz/⅓ cup) cornflour

½ teaspoon vanilla essence

350 g (12 oz/2⅓ cups) plain flour

1 Preheat oven to moderate (180°C/350°F/Gas 4). Grease an 18 x 28 cm (7 x 11¼ in) cake tin.

2 Melt the butter over low heat then leave to cool. Put the caster sugar in a bowl and sift in the icing sugar and cornflour. Beat in the cooled butter and the vanilla until pale and creamy. Stir in the sifted flour and mix until a firm dough.

3 Press mixture evenly into the prepared tin. Mark with a knife into fingers approximately 3½ x 6 cm (1¼ x 2½ in). Prick each finger several times with a fork. Bake for 30 minutes or until light golden. Cut into fingers while warm and cool in the tin.

JAM DROPS

First judged in 2001

Makes: about 30 biscuits

Six biscuits to be presented, approximately 5 cm in size. To be judged on presentation. To be presented on a tray for Branch and Group levels. At State finals a covered board and tray will be provided.

From Schedule of 2000-01

125 g (4½ oz) butter, softened
110 g (3¾ oz/½ cup) sugar
1 egg
½–1 teaspoon vanilla essence

225 g (8 oz/1½ cups) self-raising flour
Pinch of salt
Raspberry jam

1   Preheat oven to 160°C (315°F/Gas 2–3). Grease a large baking tray.

2   Beat butter and sugar until creamy, light and fluffy. Add egg and vanilla and beat again until well blended. Fold in sifted flour and salt. Form into small balls the size of a walnut, and place onto the prepared tray, allowing room to spread.

3   Make an indentation in centre of each ball and place a small quantity of jam in each. Bake for about 20 minutes until biscuits are light golden brown. Remove from oven, move positions of biscuits on tray quickly, and allow to cool on the tray and become crisp. The biscuits should measure about 5 cm (2 in) across.

GINGERBREAD PEOPLE

First judged in 1987

Makes: about 20 biscuits

Four gingerbread persons. To be iced and/or decorated.
From Schedule of 1988–89

125 g (4½ oz) butter, softened

100 g (3½ oz/½ cup, lightly packed)
   brown sugar

175 g (6 oz/½ cup) golden syrup

1 egg, separated, and 1 egg white, extra

375 g (13 oz/2½ cups) plain flour

1 tablespoon ground ginger

1 teaspoon mixed spice

1 teaspoon bicarbonate of soda

250 g (9 oz/2 cups) icing sugar

Lemon juice, to flavour

150 g (5½ oz) packet Smarties or
   chocolate buttons, to decorate

1   Preheat oven to moderate (180°C/350°F/Gas 4). Lightly grease two large
    baking trays.

2   Beat butter and brown sugar in a bowl until pale and creamy. Add the
    golden syrup and 1 egg yolk and beat until combined. Sift together the
    flour, ginger, mixed spice and bicarbonate of soda. Stir into the creamed
    mixture.

3   Turn onto a lightly floured surface and knead until smooth. Cover with
    plastic wrap and place in the fridge for 30 minutes to rest.

4   Place the dough onto a piece of baking paper and then cover with another
    piece of baking paper. Using a rolling pin, roll out the dough and cut out
    with gingerbread people shapes as needed, but keep using the baking paper.

CWA refreshment kiosk at Trangie cattle sales, 1956. Photo courtesy of CWA.

5 Move the cut shapes over to the prepared trays with a spatula/egg flip and bake for 8–10 minutes. Once baked, let cool for 10 minutes on the tray and then transfer to a covered cooling rack.

6 To make the icing, beat the 2 egg whites until they are stiff peaks, add the sifted icing sugar and combine with a few drops of lemon juice. Place into a piping bag and decorate the gingerbread people with the icing and the Smarties or chocolate buttons.

A happy competitor in *The Land* Cookery Contest, State Finals, 1961.
Photo courtesy of *The Land*.

ROCK CAKES 1

First judged in 1988

Makes: 12–15 rock cakes

Six to be displayed.
From Schedule of 2010–11

300 g (10½ oz/2 cups) self-raising flour
¼ teaspoon salt
125 g (4½ oz) butter or margarine
110 g (3¾ oz/½ cup) sugar
185 g (6½ oz/1 cup) mixed dried fruit

1 egg
½ teaspoon vanilla essence
2 tablespoons milk
Extra sugar, to sprinkle

1 Preheat oven to 200°C (400°F/Gas 6). Grease two baking trays.

2 Sift flour and salt into a bowl. Cut butter or margarine into small pieces and rub through flour until mixture resembles coarse breadcrumbs. Stir in sugar and mixed fruit. Beat egg with vanilla and milk and combine with the flour mixture, stirring just until dry ingredients are moistened.

3 Using two forks dipped in water, place heaps of mixture onto the prepared trays, leaving a space between each. Sprinkle tops with a little sugar and bake for 15 minutes or until golden and cooked through.

ROCK CAKES 2

Makes: 12–15 rock cakes

60 g (2¼ oz) butter, softened
110 g (3¾ oz/½ cup) sugar
1 egg
300 g (10½ oz/2 cups) self-raising flour
1 teaspoon ground ginger

½ teaspoon mixed spice
½ teaspoon ground cinnamon
170 g (5¾ oz/1 cup) sultanas
75 g (2¾ oz/½ cup) mixed peel
125–185 ml (4–6 fl oz/½–¾ cup) milk

1 Preheat oven to 200°C (400°F/Gas 6). Grease two baking trays.

2 Cream the butter and sugar, add the egg and beat well. Sift in the flour and spices and mix well. Add the fruit and enough of the milk to keep the mixture stiff.

3 Place spoonfuls onto the prepared trays. Bake for 15 minutes or until golden and cooked.

ROCK CAKES 3

First judged in 1988

Makes: 12–15 rock cakes

300 g (10½ oz/2 cups) self-raising flour

¼ teaspoon ground cinnamon

Pinch of salt

85 g (3 oz) butter, softened

75 g (2¾ oz/⅓ cup) caster sugar

60 g (2¼ oz/⅓ cup) sultanas or currants

40 g (1½ oz/¼ cup) mixed peel, finely chopped

1 egg

Approximately 80 ml (2½ fl oz/⅓ cup) milk

Extra caster sugar, to sprinkle

1 Preheat oven to 190°C (375°F/Gas 5). Grease two large baking trays.

2 Sift the dry ingredients into a bowl—add butter and using fingertips rub in until mixture resembles fine breadcrumbs. Stir in sugar. Add the dried fruit and peel and mix well.

3 Whisk egg and add to mixture, then add sufficient milk to make a moist but stiff consistency. If mixture is too soft, cakes will spread widely during cooking, instead of retaining shape.

4 Use 1–2 heaped tablespoons (depending on the size of cake required) to spoon mixture out in rough heaps onto the prepared trays. Leave space between each to allow for slight spreading, sprinkle cakes with extra sugar. Bake for 10–20 minutes, depending on size of cake, until cooked and golden. Loosen on tray—while hot—allow to cool on trays.

AUNT MARY'S
"EVEN-RISING"
DOES IT!

DELICIOUS CAKES EVERY TIME!

Cakes, scones and pastries are always a success when you use Aunt Mary's Baking Powder and good plain flour! Aunt Mary's special "EVEN-RISING" action begins the moment you add it to your mixture — and continues until the cake or pie is baked, deliciously light with a fine, even texture!

★ SURPRISE PACKET *FREE!*

You'll be amazed at the marvellous value of the Surprise Packet, which lucky housewives receive in exchange for 50 Seals from Aunt Mary's Baking Powder. Send your 50 Seals to Tillock & Co. Pty. Ltd., Kent and Liverpool Streets, Sydney, and your "Surprise" will come by return mail!

AUNT MARY'S
BAKING POWDER

CHOCOLATE CHIP BISCUITS 1

First judged in 2000

Makes: 30–40 biscuits

To be cooked. Approximately 5 cm in size. Six biscuits to be displayed on plate provided.
From Schedule of 1999–2000

125 g (4½ oz) butter, softened
110 g (3¾ oz/½ cup) sugar
1 teaspoon vanilla essence
1 egg, lightly whisked
170 g (5¾ oz/1 cup) chocolate chips
225 g (8 oz/1½ cups) self-raising flour

1 Preheat oven to moderate (180°C/350°F/Gas 4). Grease a large baking tray.

2 Beat the butter and sugar until white and fine. Add vanilla. Mix in whisked egg gradually. Stir in chocolate chips and sifted flour.

3 Place in small spoonfuls on the tray. Bake for 10–15 minutes. Cool on a wire rack.

CHOCOLATE CHIP BISCUITS 2

First judged in 2000

Makes: about 40 biscuits

125 g (4½ oz) butter, softened
110 g (3¾ oz/½ cup) sugar
100 g (3½ oz/½ cup, lightly packed)
  brown sugar
½ teaspoon vanilla essence
1 egg

260 g (9¼ oz/1¾ cups) self-raising flour
¼ teaspoon salt
170 g (5¾ oz/1 cup) chocolate chips
70 g (2½ oz/½ cup) peanuts, roughly
  chopped

1 Preheat oven to moderate (180°C/350°F/Gas 4). Grease a large baking tray.

2 Cream butter, sugars and vanilla. Add egg, mix well. Add sifted flour and salt, the chocolate chips and peanuts, mix until just combined.

3 Shape spoonfuls of mixture into small balls, place on the prepared tray. Bake for 10–12 minutes. Cool on a wire rack.

LOW ON EGGS?

...here's help...and how!

In these days of unavoidable shortages, Foster Clark's Creamy Custard comes to the rescue of distracted mothers who just can't imagine how to give the family their usual dessert. Flick through your handy Foster Clark's Creamy Custard recipe book and you'll find dozens of economical recipes that don't call for either eggs or fresh milk.

Write for your copy now to Foster Clark (Aust.) Ltd., Dept. R. B., Redfern, N.S.W., enclosing 2½d. postage.

Lots of flavour for little cost

FOSTER CLARK'S
Creamy Custard

F.C.4

CHOCOLATE CHIP COOKIES

First judged in 2000

Makes: 30–40 biscuits

250 g (9 oz) butter or margarine,
   softened
110 g (3¾ oz/½ cup) caster sugar
80 ml (2½ fl oz/¼ cup) condensed milk

300 g (10½ oz/2 cups) plain flour
1 teaspoon baking powder
125 g (4½ oz/¾ cup) chocolate chips

1   Preheat oven to 150°C (300°F/Gas 2). Grease a large biscuit tray.

2   Beat butter and sugar. Add condensed milk and beat well until pale and
    creamy. Sift together flour and baking powder. Add flour and baking powder
    and mix, then add chocolate chips and mix well.

3   Roll tablespoons of the mixture into balls. Place on the prepared tray.
    Press down with a fork and bake for 15 minutes. Cool on a wire rack.

Tip: This recipe can be adapted for jam drops by omitting the chocolate chips.

HEALTH COOKIES

First judged in 1999

Makes: 25–30 biscuits

Cookies to be approximately 5 cm in size, six cookies to be displayed on plate provided.
From Schedule of 1998–99

125 g (4½ oz) butter, softened

140 g (5 oz/⅔ cup) raw sugar

1 egg

1 tablespoon honey

4 teaspoons lemon juice (optional)

150 g (5½ oz/1 cup) plain wholemeal
   flour

95 g (3¼ oz/1 cup) rolled oats

75 g (2¾ oz/1 cup) wheat germ

170 g (5¾ oz/1 cup) sultanas or seeded
   raisins, chopped

155 g (5½ oz/1 cup) dried apricots,
   chopped

140 g (5 oz/1 cup) shelled peanuts

1   Preheat oven to moderate (180°C/350°F/Gas 4). Lightly grease a baking
    tray.

2   Cream together butter and sugar, add egg, mixing well, then add honey
    and lemon juice, if using. Fold in flour, oats, wheat germ, sultanas or
    raisins, apricots and peanuts, combining all ingredients well.

3   Place spoonfuls of the mixture onto the prepared tray and bake for
    15–20 minutes or until golden brown. Cool on a wire rack.

1979–80 Schedule cover. Image courtesy of the CWA.

WHEAT GERM COOKIES

First judged in 1999

Makes: 30–40 biscuits

175 g (6 oz) butter, softened
220 g (7¾ oz/1 cup) raw sugar
2 tablespoons honey
1 teaspoon vanilla essence
½ teaspoon salt
3 eggs
225 g (8 oz/1½ cups) wholemeal
  plain flour

125 g (4½ oz/1 cup) oatmeal
75 g (2¾ oz/1 cup) wheat germ
170 g (5¾ oz/1 cup) raisins, chopped
140 g (5 oz/1 cup) nuts, chopped
  (such as peanuts or walnuts)

1   Preheat oven to moderate (180°C/350°F/Gas 4). Grease a large baking tray.

2   Cream together the butter, sugar, honey, vanilla and salt until light and fluffy. Add eggs one at a time, beating well each time. Add flour, oatmeal, wheat germ, raisins and nuts. Mix together thoroughly. Stand for 10–15 minutes.

3   Drop onto the prepared tray in large spoonfuls. Flatten slightly and bake for 10–12 minutes or until a delicate brown.

RASPBERRY COCONUT SLICE

First judged in 1985

Makes: 24 pieces

Made with biscuit pastry base, jam filling and a topping of coconut mixture.

Hints to the competitor: Both slices to be presented in three layers. Base, filling and topping. Size 5 x 3¹/₂ cm. Size pieces of each slice to be presented in a covered shirt box no larger than 33 x 20 cm. Lid must be on box and sold with slices.

From Schedule of 1984–85

100 g (3½ oz/⅔ cup) plain flour
100 g (3½ oz/⅔ cup) self-raising flour
30 g (1 oz) butter, softened
55 g (2 oz/¼ cup) caster sugar
1 egg yolk
2 tablespoons water, approximately
165 g (5¾ oz/½ cup) raspberry jam

Coconut topping
270 g (9½ oz/3 cups) desiccated coconut
165 g (5¾ oz/¾ cup) caster sugar
1 egg white
1 tablespoon water
2 eggs, separated, extra
50 g (1¾ oz/⅓ cup) plain flour

1   Preheat oven to moderate (180°C/350°F/Gas 4). Lightly grease a 20 x 30 cm (8 x 12 in) cake tin, place baking paper to cover base and to extend over two opposite sides.

2   Sift flours into a bowl, rub in butter then stir in sugar. Add egg yolk and enough water to form a soft dough, press over base of the prepared tin, prick well with a fork. Bake for 12 minutes, cool.

3   To make the coconut topping, combine coconut, sugar, the egg white, water and extra egg yolks in a saucepan, stir over heat until mixture begins to stick together, do not allow coconut to brown. Cool. Beat the extra egg whites until soft peaks form. Fold sifted flour and beaten egg whites into coconut mixture.

4   Spread jam over base, press topping onto jam. Bake for about 30 minutes or until topping is well browned. Cut into squares or fingers.

PASSIONFRUIT SLICE

Makes: 24 pieces

Base

100 g (3½ oz/⅔ cup) plain flour
100 g (3½ oz/⅔ cup) self-raising flour
90 g (3 oz) butter, chilled and diced
55 g (2 oz/¼ cup) caster sugar
1 egg yolk, whisked
2 tablespoons water, approximately

Passionfruit filling

220 g (7¾ oz/1 cup) sugar
2 tablespoons custard powder
1 tablespoon butter

3 passionfruit, pulp removed
250 ml (9 fl oz/1 cup) cold water

Topping

125 ml (4½ fl oz/½ cup) condensed milk
90 g (3¼ oz/1 cup) desiccated coconut
1 teaspoon lemon essence
125 g (4½ oz/1 cup) icing sugar, sifted
35 g (1½ oz) butter, softened
Extra desiccated coconut, to serve

1   Preheat oven to moderate (180°C/350°F/Gas 4). Lightly grease a
    30 x 20 cm (12 x 8 in) slice tin and line base and sides with baking paper.

2   To make the base, sift flours into a bowl, rub in butter until mixture
    resembles fine breadcrumbs, then stir in sugar. Add egg yolk and enough
    water to form a soft dough, press over base of the prepared tin, prick well
    with a fork. Bake for 12 minutes, cool.

3   To make the passionfruit filling, place the sugar, custard powder, butter and
    passionfruit in a small saucepan and add the water. Stir over medium heat
    until thickened. Spread over the base in the tin and cool.

The "Land" Cookery Contest

ONCE again "The Land" Cookery Contest created great interest, and has become so much a part of Annual General Conference that we should feel lost indeed without it.

One's admiration goes to the people who work so hard staging and receiving and looking after the entries with such great care—the stewards: Mrs. L. G. Maitland (Barmedman), Miss Doris Foxe (Narrabri), Mrs. A. J. Murchie (Walcha), Miss A. Lugsdin (Mosman), Mrs. Cayford (Robertson), Mrs. C. C. Wilson, Mrs. W. H. Malcolm, Miss G. Winch, Mrs. C. Peck, Mrs. D. Queen and Mrs. W. A. Mills.

All the entries were of very high standard and more Branches participated than ever before. The iced cakes drew admiration from everyone, especially the little blue work basket standing on four legs, the lid half opened to show embroidery cotton, and draped from it a little mat of icing so thin that the folds fell softly. The texture looked like linen and the embroidery and lace edge were fairylike. Scissors and carded embroidery cotton lay beside the basket. A little dressing table with pink frill and all the tiny accessories was another joy.

The winning box of biscuits displayed with edging of silver paper lace, contained 18 varieties, including shortbread, chocolate macaroons, raspberry creams, shortbread fruits, strawberry buttons, ginger, almond, walnut creams, chocolate roughs, peppermint, cherry humbugs, honey biscuits, marzipan fruits, custard slices, peanut biscuits, holly leaves, cornflake daisies and sand fingers. The display was finished with a piped flower in fine gauze-like icing.

Winners of Sections were:—

Novelty Cake: 1. Mrs. G. S. Gelbart (Parkes), 2. Mrs. W. Brown (Windsor).

Special Occasion Cake: 1. Mrs. D. Evans (St. George).

Orange Cake: 1. Mrs. M. P. Langdale (Rocky Glen), 2. Mrs. C. Forsyth (Parramatta).

Light Fruit Cake: 1. Mrs. A. Wooding (Taree), 2. Mrs. A. D. Smith (South Grafton), 3. Mrs. Val Larkins (Tottenham).

Chocolate Cake: 1. Mrs. H. J. Irons (Sandigo), 2. Mrs. A. Cayford (Robertson).

Dark Fruit Cake: 1. Mrs. J. Chapple (Greenethorpe), 2. Mrs. D. T. Hayes (Albury), 3. Mrs. R. Rathbone (Griffith).

Rainbow Cake: 1. Mrs. Litchfield (Leeton), 2. Mrs. C. Gaiter (White Cliffs).

Assorted Plain Biscuits: 1. Mrs. Chris. Moore (Blighty), 2. Mrs. V. Montgomery (Taree).

Fancy Biscuits: 1. Mrs. B. Beasley (Long Jetty), 2. Mrs. N. J. Vogt (Bruton).

Sweets: 1. Mrs. P. Hammond (Hazlebrook-Woodford), 2. Mrs. O. D. Field (Pilliga).

Jelly: 1. Mrs. M. Robertson (Bemboka), 2. Mrs. D. Woods (Corrimal).

Jam: 1. Mrs. S. Townsend (South Grafton), 2. Mrs. N. Schultz (Culcairn).

Citrus: 1. Mrs. C. Baker (Emerald Hill), 2. Mrs. Mann (Eastern Suburbs).

Extract from *The Country Woman,* June 1960. Extract courtesy of the CWA.

4   To make the topping, combine all ingredients (except extra coconut) in a saucepan over medium heat, stirring until well combined. Cool, then smooth over the passionfruit filling. Sprinkle with extra coconut and cut into squares.

CHOCOLATE SLICE

First judged in 1975

Makes: 20 pieces

12 years and under 18 years.

*To be cooked, iced on top only with chocolate icing. No decoration allowed. Six pieces.
5 x 5 cm approximately, to be displayed on plate provided.*

From Schedule of 1997–98

Base and top
250 g (9 oz) milk chocolate
250 g (9 oz) dark chocolate
100 g (3½ oz) Copha

Centre
160 g (5½ oz/1 cup) chopped dates
185 g (6½ oz/1 cup, lightly packed)
  brown sugar
125 g (4½ oz) margarine
1 tablespoon honey
30 g (1 oz/1 cup) Rice Bubbles

1   Line an 18 x 28 cm (7 x 11¾ in) cake tin with foil.

2   To prepare the base, melt half of each block of chocolate with half of the Copha. Pour into tin and evenly spread. Refrigerate to set.

3   To make the centre, place all the ingredients except Rice Bubbles into a saucepan. Cook on low heat, stirring continually, for 10 minutes—careful not to burn! Allow to cool slightly, stir in Rice Bubbles. Spread over the chocolate base with back of a spoon.

4   For the top layer, melt the remaining chocolate and Copha. Pour evenly over the filling. Place in fridge until firm. Cut into small squares.

Tip: This slice freezes well.

COCONUT HONEY BARS

First judged in 1975

Makes: about 18 bars

125 g (4½ oz) butter

2 tablespoons honey

110 g (3¾ oz/½ cup) sugar

90 g (3¼ oz/1 cup) desiccated coconut

95 g (3¼ oz/1 cup) rolled oats

50 g (1¾ oz/1 cup) crushed cornflakes

Lemon icing (optional), to serve

1 Preheat oven to moderate (180°C/350°F/Gas 4). Grease an 18 x 28 cm (7 x 11¼ in) cake tin and line with baking paper. Melt butter and honey over a low heat. Combine remaining ingredients (except the lemon icing) in a bowl. Pour over the honey mixture, then mix well.

2 Press firmly into the prepared tin. Bake for 20–25 minutes or until deep golden. Cut into bars or squares while still warm and then cool in tin. Serve plain or drizzle a little lemon icing over the bars.

DATE SLICE

First judged in 1985

Makes: 16 pieces

Hints to the competitor: Pieces of slice to be presented in a covered shirt box no larger than 33 x 20 cm. Lid must be on box and sold with slices.

From Schedule of 1984–85

120 g (4¼ oz/⅔ cup) pitted dates,
  chopped
1 teaspoon finely grated lemon zest
125 ml (4 fl oz/½ cup) water
60 g (2¼ oz) butter, softened
55 g (2 oz/¼ cup) caster sugar

1 egg yolk
50 g (1¾ oz/⅓ cup) self-raising flour
50 g (1¾ oz/⅓ cup) plain flour
Pinch of salt
Lemon icing, to serve

1   Preheat oven to moderate (180°C/350°F/Gas 4). Grease a 15 cm (6 in) square cake tin and line base with baking paper.

2   Place dates in saucepan with lemon zest and water, bring to the boil and allow to simmer until soft (about 10 minutes). Cool.

3   Cream the butter and sugar and add the egg yolk. Stir in sifted flours and salt. Turn on to a floured board and knead briefly until smooth.

4   Divide mixture in half. Press one half into bottom of the prepared tin, cover with cooled dates and then top with remaining mixture, spreading to cover. Bake for 20–25 minutes. When cold, ice with lemon icing and cut into small squares.

Admiring the Array of Cakes

(Left to right) Mr E. A. Cupitt (Deputy Chairman of the County Council), Mrs J. A. Lander, Mrs W. T. Malcolm, Miss Una Clarkson (County Council) and Mr H. V. Budd, Managing Editor of *The Land* newspaper, at the 1959 State Finals. Photo courtesy of *The Land*.

HEALTH DATE AND WALNUT SLICE

First judged in 1987

Makes: about 20 pieces

Two slice varieties to be presented—six of each. Size 5 x 3¹/₂ cm. Icing optional—slice recipes to accompany entry. To be shown in a box, approximately 33 x 20 cm.

From Schedule of 1986–87

150 g (5½ oz/1 cup) wholemeal
   self-raising flour
120 g (4¼ oz/¾ cup) chopped dates
110 g (3¾ oz/½ cup) raw sugar

60 g (2¼ oz/½ cup) chopped walnuts
1 egg, whisked
60 g (2¼ oz) butter, melted

1   Preheat oven to moderate (180°C/350°F/Gas 4). Grease a 20 cm (8 in) square cake tin.

2   Combine sifted flour (including husks), dates, sugar and walnuts in a bowl.

3   Make a well in the centre. Add whisked egg and melted butter and mix well. Press mixture into the prepared tin. Bake for 30–35 minutes. Cut into slices while still hot, cool in tin.

HAZELNUT SQUARES

First judged in 2000

Makes: 24–30 squares

250 g (9 oz) unsalted butter

40 g (1½ oz) soft light brown sugar

90 g (3¼ oz/¼ cup) golden syrup

185 g (6½ oz/1⅓ cups) roasted
  hazelnuts, chopped

350 g (12 oz/2⅓ cups) plain flour

1 tablespoon baking powder

3 large eggs

Chocolate buttercream, to serve

Roasted hazelnuts, chopped, extra,
  to decorate

1   Preheat oven to moderate (180°C/350°F/Gas 4). Line a 25 x 30 cm
    (10 x 12 in) cake tin with baking paper.

2   Place the butter, sugar, golden syrup and nuts in a saucepan and melt
    gradually. Slowly bring the mixture to the boil.

3   Pour the boiling mixture into a bowl. Stir in the combined and sifted flour
    and baking powder. Stir until well combined and when cool, add the eggs.
    Mix well. Pour into the prepared tin. Bake for 25–30 minutes.

4   Cool in the tray, before decorating with chocolate buttercream and extra
    chopped hazelnuts. Cut into squares.

COFFEE SLICES

First judged in 2000

Makes: 30 slices

Must be cooked. Two varieties only, four pieces of each to be approximately 3 x 3 cm in size.
From Schedule of 1999–2000

Base

125 g (4½ oz) butter, softened

55 g (2 oz/¼ cup) caster sugar

150 g (5½ oz/1 cup) plain flour

35 g (1¼ oz/¼ cup) self-raising flour

Filling

400 g (14 oz) tin sweetened condensed
  milk

30 g (1 oz) butter

2 tablespoons golden syrup

3 teaspoons instant coffee powder

40 g (1½ oz/⅓ cup) finely chopped
  walnuts

Topping

150 g (5½ oz/1 cup) plain flour

2 teaspoons ground cinnamon

55 g (2 oz/¼ cup, firmly packed) brown
  sugar

125 g (4½ oz) butter, chopped

1 Preheat oven to moderate (180°C/350°F/Gas 4). Grease well a 25 x 30 cm (10 x 12 in) Swiss roll tin.

2 For the base, cream butter and sugar until just combined, then stir in combined and sifted flours. Mix to a firm dough. Press evenly over base of the prepared tin. Bake for 10 minutes, then spread with the filling while still hot.

3 For the filling, combine the condensed milk, butter, golden syrup and coffee in a saucepan, then stir over medium heat until mixture begins to bubble. Continue stirring briskly for about 3 minutes or until mixture is thick. Stir in walnuts. Spread over the hot base.

4 For the topping, sift flour and cinnamon into a large bowl, stir in the sugar, then rub in butter. Mix to a firm dough, gather into a ball, wrap in plastic wrap and refrigerate for 30 minutes. Grate topping evenly over surface of filling and bake for a further 10–15 minutes or until firm to the touch. Cool in tin then cut into slices.

Making the cut at the State Finals of *The Land* Cookery Competition, 1963. Photo courtesy of the CWA.

GINGER SLICE

First judged in 2003

Makes: one 20 x 30 cm (8 x 12 in) slice

Six pieces to be approximately 4 x 4 cm in size.
To be iced on top with ginger icing. Glacé ginger optional.

From Schedule of 2006–07

125 g (4½ oz) margarine

165 g (5¾ oz/¾ cup) sugar

2 tablespoons golden syrup

1 egg, whisked

300 g (10½ oz/2 cups) self-raising flour

3 teaspoons ground ginger

Chopped glacé ginger (optional)

Ginger icing, to serve

1   Preheat oven to moderate (180°C/350°F/Gas 4). Grease a 20 x 30 cm (8 x 12 in) cake tin and line base and long sides with baking paper.

2   Place margarine, sugar and golden syrup into a saucepan and melt. Allow to cool slightly.

3   Add the egg, the combined sifted flour and ground ginger and some glacé ginger, if desired. Mix well, then spread evenly into the prepared tin. Bake for 15 minutes. Ice with ginger icing when cold.

PASTRY CURRANT SLICE

First judged in 2004

Makes: about 40 pieces

Must be cooked. Six pieces to be approximately 5 x 3 x 2 cm high in size. Pastry top and bottom with currant filling. To be sprinkled on top with a little extra sugar.

From Schedule of 2004–05

150 g (5½ oz/1 cup) self-raising flour
150 g (5½ oz/1 cup) plain flour
90 g (3¼ oz) butter, chopped
1 teaspoon sugar
1 small egg
Enough milk to combine

420 g (15 oz/3 cups) currants
2 tablespoons caster sugar
1 tablespoon chopped lemon peel
Juice of 1 lemon
1 tablespoon cornflour
Extra caster sugar, to sprinkle

1 Preheat oven to moderate (180°C/350°F/Gas 4). Grease very well a 20 x 30 cm (8 x 12 in) cake tin. Sift the flours into a bowl. Rub in the butter. Add the sugar and combined egg and milk. Mix to a soft dough. Roll out half the pastry and fit into the prepared tin.

2 Put the currants, caster sugar, lemon peel and lemon juice in a saucepan. Barely cover with water and simmer for 10 minutes to soften the currants. Combine the cornflour with a little water to make a smooth paste and add to currants, stirring to thicken.

3 Cool before spreading onto pastry. Roll out remaining pastry and place over the currants. Prick with a fork. Sprinkle with a little extra sugar. Bake until golden, approximately 30 minutes. Cut into pieces while still hot and remove from tin when cool.

PEANUT CARAMEL SQUARES

First judged in 2006

Makes: about 20 squares

Must be cooked. Six pieces to be approximately 5 x 5 cm in size.

From Schedule of 2006–07

---

125 g (4½ oz) butter, softened
110 g (3¾ oz/½ cup) sugar
1 egg yolk
150 g (5½ oz/1 cup) plain flour
35 g (1¼ oz/¼ cup) self-raising flour
2 tablespoons custard powder

Topping
100 g (3½ oz/½ cup, lightly packed)
  brown sugar
1 tablespoon golden syrup
90 g (3¼ oz) butter
115 g (4 oz/¾ cup) chopped unsalted
  peanuts

1   Preheat oven to moderate (180°C/350°F/Gas 4). Grease an 18 x 28 cm (7 x 11¼ in) cake tin.

2   Cream the butter and sugar until pale and creamy, add egg yolk and mix well. Stir in sifted flours and custard powder. Mix to a firm dough. Press the mixture into the prepared tin. Bake for 15 minutes or until golden brown.

3   For the topping, place brown sugar, golden syrup and butter in a small saucepan. Stir over low heat until butter is melted and brown sugar dissolved. Simmer gently for 5 minutes. Stir in roughly chopped nuts. Spread over warm base and return to oven for 5 minutes. Allow to cool in tin. Cut into squares.

HEALTH SLICE

First judged in 1987

Makes: about 24 squares

150 g (5½ oz/1 cup) wholemeal
   self-raising flour
220 g (7¾ oz/1 cup) raw sugar
90 g (3¼ oz/1 cup) desiccated coconut
185 g (6½ oz/1 cup) mixed dried fruit
   or sultanas
6 dried apricots, chopped
250 ml (9 fl oz/1 cup) milk

1   Preheat oven to moderate (180°C/350°F/Gas 4). Grease well a 20 x 30 cm
    (8 x 12 in) slice tin.

2   Put the sifted flour (return husks to flour), sugar, coconut and dried fruit
    in a bowl and mix to combine. Stir through the milk and mix well.

3   Pour into the prepared tin and bake for 40 minutes or until cooked and
    brown on top. Cool on a wire rack and cut into squares.

MUSHROOMS

First judged in 2011

Makes: about 20

To be a sweet pastry base, filled with raspberry jam and topped with mock cream, sprinkled with nutmeg, with stem in the centre. Six to be displayed. Approximately 6 cm across.

From Schedule of 2010–11

225 g (8 oz/1½ cups) self-raising flour
125 g (4½ oz) butter, chopped
110 g (3¾ oz/½ cup) sugar
1 egg, well whisked
½ teaspoon vanilla essence

Filling

Raspberry jam
Mock cream (see page 67)
Finely grated chocolate or cocoa
  powder, to sprinkle

1   Preheat oven to moderate (180°C/350°F/Gas 4). Grease two shallow patty tins and a baking tray.

2   Sift the flour into a bowl, rub in the butter and stir in the sugar. Mix all well together. Add the egg and lastly the vanilla to form a smooth dough.

3   Roll out very thinly, and cut with a 6 cm (2½ in) biscuit cutter to fit the patty tins and bake for 10–15 minutes. To make the mushroom stems, roll the leftover dough into small pieces 6 cm (2½ in) long and 1½ cm (⅝ in) and bake for 10 minutes on the tray. Make the mock cream and refrigerate.

4   To assemble, when ready to serve, fill the centres with a scant teaspoon of the jam, fill to top with the mock cream and level off. Sprinkle with the chocolate or cocoa and place the 'stem' in the centre.

MERINGUES

To achieve success in the making of meringues is the ambition of most women. They are delectable dainties that may be served for afternoon tea or used as decoration for many sweet dishes.

They may be elaborate or simple, forced through a rose tube and made in fancy shapes and roses. Large meringues may be piled one on top of the other and joined with cream, flavoured to taste (passionfruit cream and strawberry cream are delicious). Milk puddings may be topped with meringue and decorated with cherries, etc.

New laid eggs must be used.

Stand meringues when cooked in a warm place to dry for several hours.

If the weather is warm, it is a good plan to chill the whites before whipping. If a large number of whites are being whipped it is advisable to stand in front of a window to beat them.

Meringues improve by keeping. Use an airtight tin, they should keep for weeks.

Colourings may be added to meringues: use cochineal for pink and coffee essence for coffee meringue.

Be careful when adding the sugar, a dessertspoon at a time to the beaten egg whites to fold it in, and beat it slightly after each spoonful. Always fold the sugar in, lifting the egg white from the bottom of the basin so that it is evenly blended. Do this as gently as possible, not rapidly stirring.

Icing sugar may be dredged over the meringues before putting in the oven.

If you need the meringues plain just let them remain firm and turn them over to dry. If you need them hollow turn them over when cooked on top and scoop out the soft part for filling with cream.

Coconut or almond meringues may be made by adding desiccated coconut or finely shredded blanched almonds to the mixture.

Leave an inch or more space between each meringue. Meringues may be used in a variety of ways.

They are delicious if filled with a mixture of crushed strawberries and cream or bananas and cream, while small ones make a very pretty decoration for a trifle and are also a tasty accompaniment to an ice cream of any flavour.

MERINGUES

First judged in 2011

Makes: 30–40 meringues

3 egg whites
2 teaspoons sugar
165 g (5¾ oz/¾ cup) caster sugar

1   Preheat oven to 100°C (200°F/Gas ½). Line a baking tray with baking paper.

2   Put the egg whites into a clean basin, stir in the sugar (this helps to break the egg whites up). Whip with an egg whipper (use rotary egg beater for preference) until the eggs are to a stiff froth (so firm that if the basin is held upside down the mixture will not fall out).

3   Fold in the sifted caster sugar, one spoonful at a time, until all the sugar is used up. The meringues are then shaped with the aid of a tablespoon on the baking paper.

4   Reduce oven to 80°C (165°F/Gas ¼) and bake for 1 hour or until cooked. Turn off oven and cool with the door ajar.

Tip: Some cooks use two spoons in shaping, others use the mixture through an icing tube. One of the commonest faults in meringue making is overcooking in the early stages. Meringues should be dried out rather than cooked, so place in a very cool oven.

PIKELETS

Makes: 15–20 pikelets

110 g (3¾ oz/¾ cup) *plain flour*

2 *tablespoons sugar*

1 *egg, lightly whisked*

80–100 ml (2½–3½ fl oz/
   4–5 tablespoons) *milk*

2 *teaspoons melted butter*

1 *teaspoon cream of tartar*

½ *teaspoon bicarbonate of soda*

1   Lightly grease a heavy-based frying pan. Sift the flour into a bowl and add the sugar. Combine the egg with milk and stir into dry ingredients with the butter. Stir to form a thick smooth batter and let stand for an hour or more.

2   When ready to cook, heat the frying pan. Mix cream of tartar and bicarbonate of soda in a small bowl, then add the batter and stir well. Drop spoonfuls of the mixture into the pan and cook until bubbles appear on the surface and the underside is golden. Then turn and cook the other side until golden and the pikelets are cooked through.

LEMON PIKELETS

150 g (5½ oz/1 cup) self-raising flour
Pinch of salt
2 tablespoons sugar
1 egg, whisked
Small ½ cup milk
Finely grated zest of 1 lemon
Juice of ½ lemon

1   Sift flour and salt into a bowl and add the sugar. Combine the whisked egg
    with three-quarters of the milk, the lemon zest and juice. Stir into the dry
    ingredients, beat well and make into a smooth batter, adding remaining
    milk if necessary.

2   When ready to cook, lightly grease a heavy-based frying pan and heat. Drop
    spoonfuls of the mixture into the pan and cook until bubbles appear on
    the surface and the underside is golden. Then turn and cook the other side
    until golden and the pikelets are cooked through.

SWEET TARTLETS

First judged in 1971

Tartlet Cases

Makes: about 36 tartlet cases

300 g (10½ oz/2 cups) plain flour
Pinch of salt
125 g (4½ oz) cold butter, chopped
2 tablespoons sugar
Approximately 2½ tablespoons cold water

1 Sift the flour and salt into a bowl. Rub in the butter until like fine breadcrumbs. Stir in the sugar. Mix with a little cold water to form a dough that holds together. Briefly knead on a floured board until smooth. Wrap in plastic wrap and refrigerate for 30 minutes.

2 Preheat oven to moderate (180°C/350°F/Gas 4). Roll out pastry thinly to about 3 mm (⅛ in) and cut into rounds to fit 3 teaspoon tartlet tins. Prick bases with a fork. Bake blind, with pastry cases lined with baking paper and filled with rice or split peas to hold shape, for 10 minutes. Remove paper and weights and bake for a further 5–8 minutes or until lightly golden and crisp. Cool in tartlet tins.

Lemon Meringue Tartlets

Makes: 72 tartlets

72 cooked tartlet cases (see page 162)

Lemon filling
220 g (7¾ oz/1 cup) sugar
250 ml (9 fl oz/1 cup) water
1 dessertspoon butter
Juice of 1 large or 2 small lemons

3 egg yolks
2 heaped dessertspoons arrowroot

Meringue topping
3 egg whites
165g (5¾ oz/¾ cup) sugar

1   To make the lemon filling, combine the sugar, water, butter and lemon juice in a small saucepan and stir over medium heat until the sugar dissolves. Bring to the boil over high heat and then remove from the heat.

2   Mix the arrowroot with a little water to a paste. Whisk in the egg yolks and a little of the hot syrup. Stir into the hot syrup in the saucepan. Return to the heat and stir constantly over low heat until thickened and almost simmering. Strain and set aside to cool.

3   To make the meringue topping, whisk the egg whites until soft peaks form. Gradually whisk in the sugar until the mixture is very thick and glossy.

4   To serve, preheat the grill on high. Put the tartlet cases on an oven tray, fill with the lemon filling and then top with a spoonful of meringue. Place in a moderate (180°C/350°F/Gas 4) oven until golden.

Note: There may be a little lemon filling left over. Use it to spread on toast.

Coconut and Jam Tartlets

Makes: 48 tartlets

90 g (3¼ oz/1 cup) desiccated coconut
110g (3¾ oz/½ cup) sugar
1 teaspoon baking powder
1 egg
1 tablespoon milk
320 g (11¼ oz/1 cup) raspberry or apricot jam
48 cooked tartlet cases (see page 162)

1 Preheat oven to 160°C (315°F/Gas 2–3).

2 Combine the coconut, sugar, baking powder, egg and milk. Spoon a little jam into each tartlet case and top with the coconut mixture.

3 Bake for 10–15 minutes or until lightly golden. Cool.

REMEMBER!
When cooking there is no substitute for dairy fresh MILK

Caramel Tartlets

Makes: about 36 tartlets

36 cooked tartlet cases (see page 162)

Caramel filling
240 g (8½ oz/¾ cup) condensed milk
2 tablespoons golden syrup
2 tablespoons brown sugar
20 g (¾ oz) butter

1   To make the caramel filling, stir condensed milk, golden syrup, brown sugar and butter in saucepan over medium heat until mixture comes to the boil. Reduce heat to low, cook, stirring, for 10 minutes or until thickened.

2   Allow to cool, then spoon mixture into cooked, cooled tartlet cases.

DATE CAKE

First judged in 1986

Makes: 1 x 20 cm (8 in) round or square cake

To be cooked in a 20 cm tin, iced on top only with caramel icing.
From Schedule of 1986–87

185 ml (6 fl oz/¾ cup) warm milk
¼ teaspoon bicarbonate of soda
160 g (5½ oz/1 cup) pitted dates,
   chopped
225 g (8 oz) butter, softened
220 g (7¾ oz/1 cup) caster sugar

Salt
3 eggs
90 g (3¼ oz/¾ cup) chopped walnuts
300 g (10½ oz/2 cups) plain flour
1½ teaspoons baking powder
Caramel icing, to serve

1   Preheat oven to 190°C (375°F/ Gas 5). Grease a 20 cm (8 in) round or square cake tin. Combine the milk and the bicarbonate of soda in a bowl and add dates. Soak the dates in mixture for a couple of hours.

2   Cream the butter, sugar and salt; add eggs one at a time, whisking well after each addition. Stir in the dates and milk and the walnuts. Sift together the flour and baking powder and stir into the batter until combined.

3   Spread evenly into the prepared tin. Bake for 20–25 minutes. When cold, ice with caramel icing and cut into pieces.

HONEY AND CARROT HEALTHY SLICE

First judged in 1987

Makes: 24 pieces

3 eggs, separated

1 tablespoon finely grated lemon zest

60 ml (2 fl oz/¼ cup) lemon juice

80 ml (2½ fl oz/⅓ cup) safflower oil

115 g (4 oz/⅓ cup) honey

60 g (2¼ oz/½ cup) chopped nuts
   (walnuts or mixed nuts)

155 g (5½ oz/1 cup, firmly packed)
   finely grated carrot

110 g (3¾ oz/¾ cup) wholemeal
   self-raising flour

30 g (1 oz/¼ cup) soy flour

1 Preheat oven to moderate (180°C/350°F/Gas 4). Grease an 18 x 28 cm (7 x 11¼ in) cake tin and line base with baking paper.

2 Beat together egg yolks, lemon zest and juice. Gradually beat in oil and honey until well combined. Fold in nuts, carrot and sifted flours (returning wholemeal husks to flour).

3 Whisk egg whites till soft peaks form and fold into mixture. Spread mixture evenly into the prepared tin. Bake for 30–40 minutes. Allow to cool in tin and cut into slices.

'The Land'
COOKERY CONTEST

OVER £300 IN PRIZES

CONDUCTED FOR THE COUNTRY WOMEN'S ASSOCIATION OF N.S.W.

1964–65 Schedule cover. Image courtesy of the CWA.

LOAVES, BREADS, SCONES AND MUFFINS

DRIED FIG, APPLE AND SUNFLOWER SEED BREAD
(MORNING OR AFTERNOON TEA LOAF)

First judged in 1972

Makes: 1 loaf

Suitable to be buttered. Cooked in an open or enclosed loaf tin and of good keeping quality. Even texture, well-flavoured and evenly baked.

From Schedule of 1970-71

75 g (2¾ oz/¾ cup) rolled oats

350 ml (12 fl oz) low-fat milk

300 g (10½ oz/2 cups) wholemeal self-raising flour

1 teaspoon baking powder

1 teaspoon ground cinnamon

95 g (3¼ oz/½ cup) dried figs, chopped

50 g (1¾ oz/½ cup, firmly packed) dried apples, cut into small dice

75 g (2¾ oz/⅓ cup, firmly packed) brown sugar

2 tablespoons honey

1 egg, lightly whisked

40 g (1½ oz/¼ cup) sunflower seeds, plus 2 tablespoons extra

1   Preheat oven to moderate (180°C/350°F/Gas 4). Grease a 9 x 19 cm (3½ x 7½ in) loaf tin and line base with baking paper.

2   Place oats in a bowl, pour over milk, soak for 30 minutes.

3   Sift the flour (returning husks to flour), baking powder and cinnamon into a bowl and stir in the oat mixture, the dried fruit, sugar, honey, egg and sunflower seeds. Mix well.

CWA Royal Agricultural Society Kiosk, circa 1950s. Photo courtesy of CWA.

4   Spoon the mixture into the prepared tin, level the top and sprinkle with the extra seeds. Bake for 45–50 minutes or until a skewer inserted into the centre of the loaf comes out cleanly. Allow the loaf to cool a little in the tin before turning it out onto a wire rack to cool completely.

DATE AND WALNUT ROLL 1

First judged in 1968

Makes: 2 rolls

Hints to the competitor: To be made in roll tin only.

Points to be looked for in judging: Roll should not have any large holes or tunnels and should not have hard crusts. Texture should be even and reasonably fine with fruit and nuts evenly distributed. Colour should be even and not blotchy.

From Schedule of 1967–68

1 teaspoon bicarbonate of soda

250 ml (9 fl oz/1 cup) hot water

160 g (5½ oz/1 cup) pitted dried dates

125 g (4½ oz) butter, softened

230 g (8¼ oz/1¼ cups, lightly packed) brown sugar

2 eggs, whisked

60 g (2¼ oz/½ cup) walnuts, chopped

300 g (10½ oz/2 cups) plain flour

1 teaspoon mixed spice

½ teaspoon ground cinnamon

1 Preheat oven to 170°C (325°F/Gas 3). Grease two nut roll tins very well. Dissolve bicarbonate of soda in a basin with the hot water and soak dates until soft. Cool to room temperature.

2 Beat butter and sugar to a light cream. Add whisked eggs and mix well. Add cooled date mixture and walnuts. Gradually add sifted flour and spices.

3 Spoon evenly into the prepared tins and then seal the ends. Bake for 45–50 minutes until cooked when tested with a skewer. Stand 10 minutes before removing from tins.

Tip: This roll keeps well.

DATE AND WALNUT ROLL 2

First judged in 1968

Makes: 2 rolls

160 g (5½ oz/1 cup) chopped dates
60 g (2¼ oz) butter
185 g (6½ oz/1 cup, lightly packed) brown sugar
185 ml (6 fl oz/¾ cup) water

½ teaspoon bicarbonate of soda
1 egg, lightly whisked
60 g (2¼ oz/½ cup) chopped walnuts
150 g (5½ oz/1 cup) self-raising flour
75 g (2¾ oz/½ cup) plain flour

1 Preheat oven to moderate (180°C/350°F/Gas 4). Grease two nut roll tins. Combine dates, butter, sugar and the water in a saucepan, stir constantly over heat without boiling until sugar is dissolved. Bring to the boil, remove from heat. Transfer mixture to large bowl, cool to room temperature.

2 Stir bicarbonate of soda, egg and walnuts into date mixture, then fold in the sifted flours. Spoon mixture evenly into the prepared tins and then seal the ends.

3 Bake for about 50–55 minutes or until cooked when tested with a skewer. Stand rolls in tins, with lids on, for 10 minutes. Remove lids, turn onto a covered wire rack to cool.

LAND COOKERY JUDGES SCHOOL

The LAND COOKERY COMMITTEE have arranged two Judges Schools at the C.W.A. Auditorium on THURSDAY 6TH OCTOBER, 1988 and MONDAY 21ST NOVEMBER 1988 commencing at 9.30 a.m. All you need to bring is a Notebook and Pen.

The Committee feel that an ideal number to attend the schools is 25 so please make your bookings early.

Enrolment fee will be $25 which will include a Judges Badge for each applicant who passes the set examination.

Please book your own accommodation at th C.W.A. Club and remember to send at least $18 deposit. Inform the Club that you will be attending the Land Cookery School and indicate if you are prepared to share a twin room should a single room not be available.

Members may apply for a Rail/Air N.S.W./East West Concession to attend the school. Please return the coupon below if you wish to attend.

ENROLMENT COUPON

To: 'Land' Cookery Judges School
P.O. Box 15
Potts Point 2011

Please book me for the Judges School on 6/10/88 — 21/11/88 (please indicate)

NAME...

ADDRESS ....

Tel. No (STD) ....

Enclosed is $25 enrolment fee

I require Rail — Air NSW — East West — Concession and enclose a STAMPED ADDRESSED ENVELOPE FOR THE CONCESSION AND RECEIPT

Extract from *The Country Woman*, August 1988. Extract courtesy of the CWA.

DATE AND ORANGE LOAF

First judged in 2005

Makes: 1 loaf

To be cooked in loaf tin, no icing.
From Schedule of 2004–05

---

300 g (10½ oz/2 cups) self-raising flour
1 teaspoon baking powder
165 g (5¾ oz/¾ cup) raw sugar
250 ml (9 fl oz/1 cup) boiling water
160 g (5½ oz/1 cup) chopped dates

2 teaspoons margarine or butter
1 egg, lightly whisked
1 tablespoon finely grated orange zest
2 teaspoons vanilla essence

1   Preheat oven to moderate (180°C/350°F/Gas 4). Grease a 14 x 21 cm (5½ x 8¼ in) loaf tin and line base with baking paper.

2   In a bowl sift together the flour and baking powder. Stir in the sugar. In a separate bowl combine the boiling water with the dates and margarine or butter. Leave to cool for 10 minutes, then stir in the whisked egg, orange zest and vanilla. Add to the flour mixture and stir to combine.

3   Spoon into the prepared tin. Bake for 45 minutes or until cooked when tested with a skewer. Stand 5 minutes before turning out to cool on a wire rack.

HONEY AND NUT ROLL

First judged in 1978

Makes: 2 rolls

70 g (2½ oz/1 cup) All-Bran cereal

1 tablespoon honey

250 ml (9 fl oz/1 cup) warmed milk

110 g (3¾ oz/½ cup, firmly packed)
  brown sugar

125 g (4½ oz/1 cup) chopped walnuts

150 g (5½ oz/1 cup) plain flour

1 teaspoon bicarbonate of soda

1 Preheat oven to moderate (180°C/350°F/Gas 4). Grease well two nut roll tins.

2 Put All-Bran, honey and warm milk in a large bowl and allow to stand till cold.

3 Stir through the sugar and walnuts, together with the sifted flour and bicarbonate of soda, and mix thoroughly. Spoon into the roll tins and seal the ends. Bake for about 45 minutes until cooked when tested with a skewer.

Sponge making in public at Broken Hill. Darling River Group *The Land* Cookery Group Finals. Mrs G. E. Carr won the Scone competition and Mrs G. E. Souter, Sponge Cake, July 1958. Photo courtesy of *The Land*.

Better REFRIGERATION

with LAUREL KEROSENE

Your refrigerator will operate more efficiently and economically on Laurel — the cleanest, purest kerosene you can buy. Laurel burns steadily to the last drop, without smoke or smell. It is the perfect kerosene for refrigeration.

VACUUM OIL COMPANY PTY. LTD. (Incorp. in Aust.)

L4642

LAUREL
THE PERFECT ALL - PURPOSE KEROSENE

For Lighting, Heating, Cooking, Cleaning, Freezing

CARROT AND NUT LOAF

First judged in 1987

Makes: 1 loaf

Made in loaf tin. IMPORTANT: Should be of good keeping quality, suitable to be buttered for afternoon tea. Should be evenly baked and not peaked.

From Schedule of 1985–86

150 g (5½ oz/1 cup) wholemeal plain flour

½ teaspoon baking powder

½ teaspoon bicarbonate of soda

½ teaspoon mixed spice

½ teaspoon salt

2 eggs

220 g (7¾ oz/1 cup) raw sugar

185 ml (6 fl oz/¾ cup) vegetable oil

1 teaspoon vanilla essence

235 g (8½ oz/1½ cups, firmly packed) grated carrot

60 g (2¼ oz/½ cup) finely chopped walnuts or pecan nuts

130 g (4¾ oz/¾ cup) sultanas (optional)

1   Preheat oven to moderate (180°C/350°F/Gas 4). Grease a 9 x 19 cm (3½ x 7½ in) loaf tin and line base with baking paper. Sift together the flour (returning the husks to the flour), baking powder and bicarbonate of soda, mixed spice and salt.

2   Combine eggs, sugar, oil and vanilla in a mixing bowl. Add the sifted dry ingredients to the bowl and beat all together—but do not overbeat. Stir in grated carrot and nuts and sultanas, if using.

3   Pour mixture into the prepared tin. Bake for about 1 hour or until cooked when tested with a skewer.

CARROT GINGERBREAD LOAF

First judged in 2007

Makes: 1 loaf

To be cooked in loaf tin. Lemon icing on top. No decoration.
From Schedule of 2007–08

185 g (6½ oz) butter

175 g (6 oz/½ cup) golden syrup

110 g (3¾ oz/½ cup, firmly packed) brown sugar

125 ml (4 fl oz/½ cup) water

155 g (5½ oz/1 cup, firmly packed) roughly grated carrot

1 teaspoon bicarbonate of soda

225 g (8 oz/1½ cups) plain flour

110 g (3¾ oz/¾ cup) self-raising flour

1 tablespoon ground ginger

Lemon icing, to serve

1 Preheat oven to moderate (180°C/350°F/Gas 4). Grease an 11 x 21 cm (4¼ x 8¼ in) loaf tin and line base with baking paper.

2 Combine butter, golden syrup and sugar in a saucepan with the water. Stir over medium heat until butter is melted and sugar dissolved. Bring to boil, remove from heat, and stir in carrot and bicarbonate of soda. Set aside for about 30 minutes.

3 Stir in sifted flours and ginger, beat until smooth. Pour mixture into the prepared tin. Bake for about 45 minutes or until cooked when tested. When cold, ice top of cake.

BOILED CARROT LOAF

First judged in 2009

Makes: 1 loaf

To be cooked in loaf tin. No icing.

From Schedule of 2008–09

---

155 g (5½ oz/1 cup, firmly packed)
  grated carrot

130 g (4¾ oz/¾ cup) chopped raisins

165 g (5¾ oz/¾ cup) caster sugar

30 g (1 oz) butter

½ teaspoon ground cinnamon

½ teaspoon ground nutmeg

185 ml (6 fl oz/¾ cup) water

110 g (3¾ oz/¾ cup) self-raising flour

110 g (3¾ oz/¾ cup) plain flour

½ teaspoon bicarbonate of soda

60 g (2¼ oz/½ cup) chopped walnuts

1　Preheat oven to 160°C (315°F/Gas 2–3). Grease a 9 x 19 cm (3½ x 7½ in) loaf tin and line base with baking paper.

2　Combine carrot, raisins, sugar, butter, cinnamon and nutmeg in a saucepan, add the water and stir over heat without boiling until sugar is dissolved. Bring to the boil, reduce heat, cover and simmer for 10 minutes. Cool to room temperature.

3　Sift the flours together. Stir in half the sifted flours and the bicarbonate of soda, then remaining flour and walnuts. Spread into the prepared tin. Bake for about 1 hour or until cooked. Stand 5 minutes before turning out.

GINGERBREAD

First judged in 1975

Makes: 1 loaf

110 g (3¾ oz/¾ cup) plain flour

35 g (1¼ oz/¼ cup) self-raising flour

½ teaspoon bicarbonate of soda

1 teaspoon ground ginger

¼ teaspoon ground cinnamon

¼ teaspoon mixed spice

110 g (3¾ oz/½ cup) caster sugar

1 egg, lightly whisked

125 ml (4 fl oz/½ cup) milk

60 g (2¼ oz) butter

175 g (6 oz/½ cup) treacle

Lemon icing

60 g (2¼ oz) butter, softened

1 teaspoon finely grated lemon zest

125 g (4½ oz/1 cup) icing sugar

Approximately 2 teaspoons lemon
  juice, to taste

1 Preheat oven to moderate (180°C/350°F/Gas 4). Grease a 14 x 21 cm (5½ x 8¼ in) loaf tin and line base with baking paper.

2 Sift the flours, bicarbonate of soda, spices and sugar into a large bowl. Stir in the combined egg and milk.

3 Combine the butter and treacle in a saucepan, and stir constantly over low–moderate heat, without boiling, until butter is melted. Stir this hot mixture into the flour mixture.

4   Pour into the prepared tin. Bake for about 50 minutes. Stand for 5 minutes before turning out onto a wire rack to cool.

5   To make the icing, beat the butter and lemon zest in a small bowl until pale and creamy. Gradually beat in the sifted icing sugar and enough lemon juice to get the taste and consistency you want. Spread over the top of the cooled cake.

DATE LOAF

First judged in 1975

Makes: 1 loaf

Date loaf suitable to be buttered and of good keeping quality. Even texture, well flavoured and evenly baked in an open loaf tin.

From Schedule of 1978-79

160 g (5½ oz/1 cup) chopped dates
250 ml (9 fl oz/1 cup) boiling water
½ teaspoon bicarbonate of soda
1 tablespoon butter, softened
150 g (5½ oz/¾ cup, lightly packed)
  brown sugar

1 egg
225 g (8 oz/1½ cups) self-raising flour
1 teaspoon ground cinnamon

1   Preheat oven to 170°C (325°F/Gas 3). Grease a 9 x 19 cm (3½ x 7½ in) loaf tin and line base with baking paper.

2   Soak dates in the boiling water with bicarbonate of soda, until softened. Cool to room temperature.

3   Cream butter with sugar. Add egg and beat well. Add cooled dates and water then fold in the combined and sifted flour and cinnamon. Pour into the prepared tin and bake for about 1 hour.

APRICOT LOAF

First judged in 1980

Makes: 1 loaf

To be cooked in loaf tin, no nuts allowed. Must be good keeping quality, presented un-iced.
From Schedule of 1988–89

120 g (4¼ oz/⅔ cup) dried apricots

250 ml (9 fl oz/1 cup) boiling water

125 g (4½ oz) butter, softened

220 g (7¾ oz/1 cup) caster sugar

1 teaspoon vanilla essence or finely
   grated lemon zest

2 eggs

185 g (6½ oz/1¼ cups) plain flour

150 g (5½ oz/1 cup) self-raising flour

1   Preheat oven to moderate (180°C/350°F/Gas 4). Grease a 13 x 23 cm (5 x 9 in) loaf tin and line base with baking paper.

2   Cut apricots with scissors, cover with the boiling water, leave till cold. Cream butter, sugar and vanilla or lemon zest, then add eggs one at a time and beat well. Sift the flours several times and fold into the mixture. Drain the apricots well and stir into the mixture, mix well and lightly.

3   Spoon mixture into the prepared tin, release air bubbles by tapping lightly on bench. Bake for 1½ hours or until cooked when tested.

APRICOT AND SULTANA LOAF

First judged in 2007

Makes: 1 loaf

18 years and under. To be cooked in loaf tin. No icing.
From Schedule of 2006–07

125 g (4½ oz) butter, softened

150 g (5½ oz/⅔ cup, firmly packed) brown sugar

2 eggs

130 g (4 ¾ oz/½ cup) plain yoghurt

65 g (2¼ oz/½ cup) roughly chopped dried apricots

85 g (3 oz/½ cup) sultanas

185 g (6½ oz/1¼ cups) self-raising flour

1   Preheat oven to moderate (180°C/350°F/Gas 4). Grease a 9 x 19 cm (3½ x 7½ in) loaf tin and line base with baking paper.

2   Beat butter and sugar in a small bowl with an electric mixer until pale and creamy. Add eggs, one at a time, beating until combined after each addition.

3   Transfer mixture to a larger bowl. Stir in the yoghurt, apricots and sultanas; then stir through the sifted flour and mix well.

4   Spoon into the prepared tin. Bake for about 1 hour or until cooked when tested. (Cover top loosely with foil during cooking if over browning.) Stand loaf in the tin for 5 minutes, turn out onto a wire rack to cool.

DRIED APRICOT LOAF

First judged in 2007

Makes: 1 loaf

220 g (7¾ oz/1 cup) sugar

130 g (4¾ oz/1 cup) chopped dried
  apricots

85 g (3 oz/½ cup) sultanas

75 g (2¾ oz/½ cup) currants

60 g (2¼ oz) butter

250 ml (9 fl oz/1 cup) boiling water

1 egg, whisked

1 apple, grated

300 g (10½ oz/2 cups) self-raising flour

1 Preheat oven to moderate (180°C/350°F/Gas 4). Grease an 11 x 21 cm
   (4¼ x 8¼ in) (base measurement) loaf tin and line base with baking paper.

2 Put the sugar, apricots, sultanas, currants and butter into a bowl and pour
   over the boiling water. Allow to cool. Mix in the whisked egg and apple then
   stir through the sifted flour.

3 Put into the prepared tin. Bake for 40–45 minutes or until cooked when
   tested.

'Land' cookery contest attracts many entries of outstanding excellence

Mrs H. J. Brazel, from Niangala, looks hopeful as she takes a batch of scones from the oven during the closing stages of this year's *The Land* Cookery finals at Sydney Town Hall, June 1971. Photo courtesy of *The Land*.

APRICOT HEALTH LOAF

First judged in 1981

Makes: 1 loaf

125 g (4½ oz/1 cup) chopped walnuts
or almonds

155 g (5½ oz/1 cup) dried apricot
halves, chopped

170 g (5¾ oz/1 cup) sultanas

165 g (5¾ oz/¾ cup) raw sugar

70 g (2½ oz/1 cup) All-Bran cereal

375 ml (13 fl oz/1½ cups) milk

225 g (8 oz/1½ cups) wholemeal
self-raising flour (or 225 g/8 oz/
1½ cups wholemeal plain flour and
1½ teaspoons baking powder)

1 Combine nuts, chopped apricots and sultanas, sugar and All-Bran with
   milk and allow to stand for 2 hours.

2 Preheat oven to moderate (180°C/350°F/Gas 4). Grease an 11 x 21 cm
   (4¼ x 8¼ in) loaf tin and line base with baking paper.

3 Fold the flour (and baking powder if using plain flour) into the fruit
   mixture. Mix well and pour into the prepared tin. Bake for 1 hour or until
   cooked when tested with a skewer.

HEALTH LOAF

First judged in 1981

Makes: 1 loaf

150 g (5½ oz/1 cup) wholemeal
  self-raising flour
220 g (7¾ oz/1 cup) sugar
90 g (3¼ oz/1 cup) desiccated coconut
250 ml (9 fl oz/1 cup) milk
185 g (6½ oz/1 cup) fruit medley (or
  your choice of mixed dried fruits)

1 Preheat oven to moderate (180°C/350°F/Gas 4). Grease a 9 x 19 cm
   (3½ x 7½ in) loaf tin and line base with baking paper.

2 Combine all ingredients together, mix well.

3 Spoon into the prepared tin. Bake for 50 minutes or until cooked when
   tested with a skewer. Cool. Serve plain or buttered.

FRUIT 'N' NUT HEALTH ROLL

First judged in 1999

Makes: 2 rolls

Not to be trimmed.
From Schedule of 1998–99

---

185 g (6½ oz/1 cup) mixed dried fruit

60 g (2¼ oz) butter

220 g (7¾ oz/1 cup, firmly packed)
  brown sugar

185 ml (6 fl oz/¾ cup) water

½ teaspoon bicarbonate of soda

1 egg, lightly whisked

60 g (2¼ oz/½ cup) chopped walnuts

150 g (5½ oz/1 cup) wholemeal
  self-raising flour

75 g (2¾ oz/½ cup) plain flour

1   Preheat oven to moderate (180°C/350°F/Gas 4). Grease well two nut roll tins.

2   Combine fruit, butter, sugar and the water in a saucepan, stir constantly over heat without boiling until sugar is dissolved. Bring to the boil, then remove from the heat. Transfer mixture to a large bowl, cool to room temperature.

3   Stir bicarbonate of soda, egg and walnuts into fruit mixture then combined and sifted flours (return husks to flour).

4   Spoon mixture evenly into the prepared tins and then seal the ends. Bake for about 1 hour or until cooked when tested with a skewer. Stand rolls in tins, with lids on, for 10 minutes. Remove lids then turn out onto a wire rack to cool.

It's Perfect!
—thanks to
Aunt Mary's
Baking Powder

Send
One Shilling & Twopence
to Tillock & Co. Pty. Ltd.
Sydney
for a copy of
Aunt Mary's
Cookery Book

Save 50 parchment seals (under the lid) from the tins of Aunt Mary's Baking Powder and send them to Tillock & Co. Pty. Ltd., Kent & Liverpool Sts., Sydney, with your name and address and you will receive a Handsome Surprise Packet FREE!

FRUIT AND WALNUT HEALTH ROLL

First judged in 1967

Makes: 2 nut rolls

255 g (9 oz/1½ cups) raisins
80 g (2¾ oz/½ cup) dried apricots
90 g (3¼ oz/¾ cup) chopped walnuts
100 g (3½ oz/½ cup, lightly packed)
  brown sugar

1 teaspoon bicarbonate of soda
250 ml (9 fl oz/1 cup) evaporated milk
1 egg, lightly whisked
300 g (10½ oz/2 cups) plain wholemeal
  flour

1   Preheat oven to moderate (180°C/350°F/Gas 4). Grease well two nut roll
    tins.

2   Place the raisins, apricots, walnuts, sugar and bicarbonate of soda in a
    bowl. Stir in evaporated milk and whisked egg, mixing thoroughly. Sift flour
    (returning husks to the flour) and stir through the mixture.

3   Spoon evenly into the prepared tins. Bake with lids on for 45 minutes.
    Stand rolls in tins with lids on for 10 minutes. Remove the lids and turn
    out onto a wire rack to cool.

BANANA, ORANGE AND DATE HEALTH LOAF

First judged in 1981

Makes: 1 loaf

90 g (3¼ oz) butter, softened

2 teaspoons finely grated orange zest

110 g (3¾ oz/½ cup) raw sugar

2 eggs

240 g (8¾ oz/1 cup) mashed ripe banana

120 g (4¼ oz/¾ cup) chopped dates

300 g (10½ oz/2 cups) wholemeal self-raising flour

125 ml (4 fl oz/½ cup) orange juice

1 Preheat oven to moderate (180°C/350°F/Gas 4). Grease a 9 x 19 cm (3½ x 7½ in) loaf tin and line base and sides with baking paper.

2 Cream butter, orange zest and sugar in a small bowl until light and fluffy, beat in eggs one at a time, add banana, beat until combined.

3 Transfer mixture to a large bowl, stir in dates. In a separate bowl, sift the flour (returning the husks to the flour). Add half the flour to the mixture, then half the orange juice, then stir in the remaining flour and orange juice; stir until smooth.

4 Spread into the prepared tin. Bake for about 1 hour. Stand 10 minutes before turning out to cool.

Auctioneering the cakes: Miss D. Foxe (Narrabri), Mrs W. H. Cullen, Mrs Davis (Gunning), and Mr Bob Pollard of Station 2UE, who acted as auctioneer at State Finals, 1951. Photo courtesy of *The Land*.

SWEET BUN LOAF

(EGGLESS)

First judged in 2005

Makes: 1 loaf

Un-iced. To be cooked in loaf tin.
From Schedule of 2004–05

300 g (10½ oz/2 cups) self-raising
  flour, sifted
170 ml (5½ fl oz) milk or water
2 tablespoons golden syrup
2 tablespoons sultanas or mixed peel
1 tablespoon marmalade

1 Preheat oven to moderate (180°C/350°F/Gas 4). Grease a 9 x 19 cm (3½ x 7½ in) loaf tin and line base with baking paper.

2 Combine all ingredients in a bowl and mix well.

3 Spoon into the prepared tin and bake for 45 minutes or until cooked when tested with a skewer. Wrap in a tea towel while still hot and leave until next day before slicing. Enjoy plain or buttered.

DATE PINWHEELS

First judged in 2008

Makes: 35–40 pinwheels

215 g (7½ oz/1⅓ cups) chopped dates

2 tablespoons brown sugar

1 tablespoon lemon juice

Finely grated zest of 1 lemon

2 tablespoons water

30 g (1 oz/¼ cup) finely chopped
  walnuts

125 g (4½ oz) butter, softened

55 g (2 oz/¼ cup) caster sugar

100 g (3½ oz/½ cup, lightly packed)
  brown sugar, extra

1 egg

½ teaspoon vanilla essence

300 g (10½ oz/2 cups) plain flour

½ teaspoon bicarbonate of soda

Pinch of salt

1 Cook dates, brown sugar, lemon juice, zest and the water in a saucepan over low heat until soft, then beat well. Add walnuts, leave to cool.

2 Cream the butter, caster sugar and extra brown sugar then beat in the egg and vanilla. Sift together the flour, bicarbonate of soda and salt and fold into the creamed mixture. Halve the dough and wrap in plastic wrap. Allow to chill for 30 minutes, then knead briefly until smooth.

3 Roll each half of the dough to an oblong shape 6 mm (¼ in) thick. Spread with date mixture. Roll like a Swiss roll, no more than 4 cm (1½ in) thick. Wrap in plastic wrap and refrigerate overnight.

4 Preheat oven to moderate (180°C/350°F/Gas 4). Grease a large baking tray. Cut the rolls into 1 cm (½ in) thick slices and put on tray. Bake for 8–10 minutes. Cool on a wire rack.

DAMPER

First judged in 1977

Makes: 1 round loaf

450 g (1 lb/3 cups) self-raising flour
1 teaspoon salt
310 ml (10¾ fl oz/1¼ cups) milk
  (skimmed milk best, not boiled milk)

1   Preheat oven to 220°C (425°F/Gas 7). Lightly flour a baking tray.

2   Sift the flour and salt into a bowl. Add the milk all at once and mix with a knife to a good dough, which leaves the sides of the basin clean.

3   Turn the dough out and lightly knead into a smooth round. Place on the tray. Cut a cross in the dough or prick the top. Bake for 30 minutes on the bottom shelf of the oven.

Apple Pie Order

When the family orders pie — bake and serve in Agee Pyrex. It's easier — it's more attractive .. it's economical.

STRAIGHT from the oven to the table . . . golden pastry, as light as a feather—a pie perfectly cooked and attractively enthroned on a glistening Pyrex dish . . . that's pie as it SHOULD be! Wise housewives are using more and more Pyrex for cooking . . . it's economical . . . it's time and labour saving . . . it's *modern!* No need to wait any longer before beginning to equip *your* kitchen with this eye-pleasing, long-lasting and infinitely useful ovenware which is tableware as well.

AGEE PYREX
MARKETED BY CROWN CRYSTAL GLASS PTY. LTD.
Makers of vitally necessary dispensary, laboratory and clinical glassware for use by the fighting forces.

WHOLEMEAL BREAD

First judged in 1982

Makes: 2 loaves

900 g (2 lb/6 cups) wholemeal
  plain flour
450 g (1 lb/3 cups) plain flour
125 g (4½ oz) butter, chopped
30 g (1 oz) fresh yeast (or 15 g/½ oz
  dried yeast)

½ teaspoon sugar
250 ml (9 fl oz/1 cup) lukewarm milk
125 ml (4 fl oz/½ cup) lukewarm water
1½ teaspoons salt

1   Lightly flour a large baking tray or grease two large bread tins. Place the
    wholemeal and plain sifted flour in a large warm basin, rub in the butter
    using fingers. Put the yeast and sugar in a basin or jug. Add the warmed
    milk and warm water and mix well together.

2   Make a hollow in the centre of the flour and pour in the liquid, sprinkle
    salt on the flour around the edges of the hollow. Stir with a wooden spoon
    until flour is well mixed.

3   Cover with a clean tea towel and allow to stand in a warm spot till double
    its size (about 1 hour). Turn on to a lightly floured board. Knead till smooth
    and elastic (about 10 minutes).

4   Preheat oven to 220°C (425°F/Gas 7). Shape into two freeform loaves,
    or shape and put into the prepared bread tins. Stand in a warm place for
    10 minutes, then bake for 20 minutes. Reduce the heat to moderate
    (180°C/350°F/Gas 4) and bake for a further 45 minutes. Turn out onto
    a wire rack and cover with a clean cloth to cool.

1969–70 Schedule cover. Image courtesy of the CWA.

PRIZE-WINNING SCONES

First judged in 1972

Makes: about 12–15 scones

450 g (1 lb/3 cups) plain flour

60 g (2¼ oz/½ cup) icing sugar

2 teaspoons cream of tartar

1 teaspoon bicarbonate of soda

½ teaspoon salt

60 g (2¼ oz) chilled butter, cubed

Approximately 310 ml (10¾ fl oz/ 1¼ cups) milk

1   Preheat oven to 200°C (400°F/Gas 6). Heat a baking tray in the oven.

2   Sift the flour, icing sugar, cream of tartar, bicarbonate of soda and salt together three times. Put in a bowl and rub in the butter. Make a well in the centre. Pour into the well about three-quarters of the milk. Use a knife to mix the milk through the flour to mix to a soft dough, adding remaining milk if needed to form a soft dough.

3   Turn out onto a floured board and lightly knead. The mixture should be handled as lightly as possible and patted into shape with your hands.

4   Cut the dough into shapes as desired and brush over with a little milk. Lightly flour the heated tray and place the scones on the tray. Bake for 12–15 minutes or until a rich golden brown.

Tip: Add a whisked egg with the milk if liked but reduce milk to about 250 ml (9 fl oz/1 cup).

PLAIN SCONES

First judged in 1970

Makes: about 12 scones

The best 12 scones from a 1 lb white flour mixture to be entered using a plain basic scone recipe, without eggs. A round cutter of 2 inch diameter should be used. (Several brands of flour will be available at the Finals if desired. If competitors prefer to supply their own flour, it must be brought in unopened packets.) Points to be looked for in judging: Fine texture, even rising, golden brown on top and bottom. Scones should be placed on a baking tray, close but not touching. No marks or flour should appear on the surfaces.

All these points, together with palatability, will be looked for in judging.

From Schedule of 1969–70

450 g (1 lb/3 cups) plain flour
2 teaspoons baking powder
Salt
1 tablespoon butter, softened
150 ml (5 fl oz) milk
150 ml (5 fl oz) water

1   Preheat oven to 220°C (425°F/Gas 7). Lightly flour a baking tray.

2   Sift flour, baking powder and salt together into a bowl, then rub in the butter with the tips of the fingers. Using a knife, lightly mix in the milk and water until it forms a smooth dough.

3   Turn dough out onto a floured board and lightly knead. Roll out to about 1.5 cm (⅝ in) thick, then cut into 5 cm (2 in) rounds. Place on the prepared tray and bake for 7–10 minutes.

BANANA MUFFINS

First judged in 2007

Makes: 12 muffins

300 g (10½ oz/2 cups) self-raising flour

130 g (4¾ oz/1 cup) oat bran

165 g (5¾ oz/¾ cup) caster sugar

60 g (2¼ oz) butter, melted

185 ml (6 fl oz/¾ cup) milk

2 eggs, lightly whisked

240 g (8¾ oz/1 cup) mashed ripe banana

1   Preheat oven to 200°C (400°F/Gas 6). Grease a 12-hole (125 ml/4 fl oz/ ½ cup) muffin tin.

2   Sift flour into a large bowl, add the oat bran and the sugar and stir well. Make a well in the centre of the mixture. Add combined butter, milk, eggs and banana all at once. Using a wooden or metal spoon, stir until just mixed. Do not overbeat; the batter should remain lumpy.

3   Spoon mixture evenly into the prepared muffin tin holes. Bake for 15 minutes or until risen and brown.

Make
SCONES LIGHT AS A FEATHER!

Scones, cakes and pastries always come out a success when you use Aunt Mary's Baking Powder and good plain flour! The special "EVEN-RISING" action of Aunt Mary's begins the moment you add it to your mixture — and continues until the cake or pie is baked, deliciously light, with a fine even texture!

Aunt Mary's has won thousands of cake-baking competitions for lucky housewives — it must be good!

★AUNT MARY'S SURPRISE PACKET!

Send 50 Seals from under the lids of Aunt Mary's Baking Powder to Tillock & Co. Pty. Ltd., Kent and Liverpool Streets, Sydney — and your Surprise Packet will come by return mail!

AUNT MARY'S
BAKING POWDER

BANANA DATE MUFFINS

First judged in 2007

Makes: 12 muffins

Competitors 12 years and under. To be cooked in regular muffin tins. Six muffins to be displayed on plate provided.

From Schedule of 2006–07

300 g (10½ oz/2 cups) self-raising flour

1 teaspoon mixed spice

110 g (3¾ oz/½ cup, firmly packed) brown sugar

160 g (5½ oz/1 cup) chopped dates

240 g (8¾ oz/1 cup) mashed banana (approximately 2 large, over-ripe bananas)

3 eggs, lightly whisked

80 ml (2½ fl oz/⅓ cup) vegetable oil

80 ml (2½ fl oz/⅓ cup) buttermilk

1   Preheat oven to 200°C (400°F/Gas 6). Grease a 12-hole (125 ml/4 fl oz/ ½ cup) muffin tin.

2   Sift flour and spice into a large bowl, add the sugar and dates and stir well. Make a well in the centre of the mixture. Add combined banana, eggs, oil and buttermilk all at once. Using a wooden or metal spoon, stir until just mixed. Do not overbeat; the batter should remain lumpy.

3   Spoon mixture evenly into the prepared muffin tin holes. Bake for 15–20 minutes or until risen and brown.

— "LAND" COOKERY CONTEST —

The "Land" Cookery Contest conducted by the "Land" Newspaper for the Country Women's Association Seaside Homes' Appeal, again this year was most successful. This competition has now been held for four years in succession, and causes great interest all through the countryside.

Cakes are first judged in Branch competitions and the winners of the Branches are then competitors in the Group semi-finals, while the winners from each Group compete in the State finals in Sydney.

This year the final prize winners were as follows:—

Section 1.

Dark Fruit Cake:
1. Mrs. N. C. Schomberg, Bega.
2. Mrs. L. C. Holgate, Matong.
3. Mrs. C. E. Campbell, Stroud.

Light Fruit Cake:
1. Mrs. G. Pascall, Western Suburbs.
2. Mrs. N. McIntyre, Walla Walla.
3. Mrs. C. Searle, Singleton.

Section 2.

Rainbow Cake:
1. Mrs. G. Pascall, Western Suburbs.
2. Mrs. A. F. Pankhurst, Branxton-Greta.

Orange Cake:
1. Mrs. G. A. Devenish, Neville.
2. Mrs. A. Davis, Branxton-Greta.

Chocolate Cake:
1. Mrs. G. McEwan, Richmond.
2. Mrs. G. Pascall, Western Suburbs.

Section 3.

Fancy Biscuits:
1. Mrs. C. Baker, Emerald Hill.
2. Mrs. E. J. Hancock, Coolamon.

Plain Biscuits:
1. Mrs. Wooding, Dee Why.
2. Mrs. Hamblin, Matong.

Section 4.

Jam:
1. Mrs. A. McManus, Grattai.
2. Mrs. J. Morehead, Mulgoa.

Jelly:
1. Mrs. L. M. Lemon, Weethalle.
2. Mrs. R. Godden, Albury.

The thanks of the Association go to the organisers of this contest, the "Land" Newspaper, and to Mrs. Vera Hamilton, who worked so hard for its success; to judges and stewards, and last, but certainly not least, to all those members who competed in Branch and Group contests. Congratulations to the winners!

Extract from *The Country Woman*, June 1954. Extract courtesy of the CWA.

SWEET MUFFINS

First judged in 2000

Makes: 12 muffins

To be cooked. Six muffins to be displayed on a plate provided.
From Schedule of 1999–2000

300 g (10½ oz/2 cups) plain flour
3 teaspoons baking powder
½ teaspoon salt
60 g (2¼ oz) butter, softened
110 g (3¾ oz/½ cup) caster sugar
250 ml (9 fl oz/1 cup) low-fat milk
1 apple, peeled, cored and chopped

1   Preheat oven to 200°C (400°F/Gas 6). Lightly grease a 12-hole (125 ml/ 4 fl oz/½ cup) muffin tin, or line with paper muffin cup cases.

2   In a bowl, sift together the flour, baking powder and salt. In a separate bowl, beat together the butter and sugar until pale and creamy. Stir the flour mixture into the butter mixture alternately with the milk. Fold in the apple.

3   Spoon batter into the prepared muffin tin holes. Bake for 20–25 minutes or until a toothpick inserted into the centre of a muffin comes out clean. Cool on a wire rack.

INDEX